Assisted Suicide & Euthanasia
past & present

J.C. Willke, MD
with Frederic Wertham, MD
Cathleen Cleaver, JD
Edward Grant, JD
Mark Rothe, JD

Chapter 2 was originally published under the auspices of The Family Research Council of Washington, DC. Chapters 3 and 4 have been published under the title of *The German Euthanasia Program* by Hayes Publishing Company in two editions in 1980 and 1983. Originally these were published as chapters 8 and 9 in *A Sign for Cain* by the Macmillan Company of New York and Collier-Macmillan Limited of London. Copyright 1966 by Fredric Wertham. Paperback editions of *A Sign for Cain* were published by the Warner Paperback Library, New York, in 1969 and 1973. Reprinted with the permission of The Macmillan Company, New York.

Copyright © 1998
Hayes Publishing Co.

ISBN 910728-22-4

Hayes Publishing Co., Inc.
6304 Hamilton Ave. Cincinnati, OH 45224
Ph: (513) 681-7559   Ph/Fax: (513) 681-9298
e-mail: hayespub@aol.com

ASSISTED SUICIDE AND EUTHANASIA
Past and Present

Assisted Suicide & Euthanasia – past & present

FOREWARD

Dr. Frederick Wertham first published *A Sign For Cain* in 1966. Later, two of the chapters contained in this book were published separately under the title, *The German Euthanasia Program*. The issue of euthanasia at that time was principally historical. The Holocaust was a horror that could never be repeated. The knowledge of its small beginnings, how it had developed, and the ultimate overwhelming tragedy it became, was knowledge available to anyone interested. Certainly, nothing remotely like this could ever happen again. Civilized nations surely would not begin to walk a path similar to that walked in Germany in the 1920s and '30s.

But history can repeat. Today we are living, once again, in the midst of a "culture of death". This time it began with abortion. Human life was no longer regarded as sacred, no longer protected in his or her mother's womb. As slavery had done in America 150 years earlier, so it was that abortion was to slowly corrode the conscience of a nation. If killing was to be allowed before birth, why not, for the same reasons, after birth? If killing was allowed for a variety of social and economic reasons in the early months of life, why not a painless "termination", for all those same reasons, in the last months of life?

Euthanasia would not suddenly arrive full bloom but had to come through a gradual process. Advance directives, or so called "living wills", were the beginning. Following this, attempts to jump directly into doctors killing patients were not successful in the States of California, Oregon and Washington, and so the approach of "assisted suicide" was tried. This ruse has since also failed in Australia and has been rejected unanimously by the United States Supreme Court but approved in Oregon. The controversy is only beginning. The main battles still lie ahead.

We begin with an overview of euthanasia as such. Then an analysis of the events leading up to the German Euthanasia Program by Cathy Cleaver, Edward Grant and Mark Rothe. Following Dr. Wertham's excellent narrative on the Holocaust in Chapters III and IV, an historical analysis of medical and ethical oaths is presented. After this, your author examines the Dutch Euthanasia Program and then contemporary "assisted suicide", listing the reasons given for it and providing brief answers. Finally, a look at the medical profession today, the 1997 U.S. Supreme Court decision, the Oregon happening and what your author proposes as answers to the push for euthanasia.

It is our hope that this new publication, along with Wertham's classical chapters, will be of help to those interested in this latest threat to human life.

J. C. Willke, M.D.

CHAPTER I
EUTHANASIA

Words are important. It is common, when people approach this subject, to look for the meaning of the word "euthanasia" and to recall that its translation means "good death". This should be ignored and rejected, as it has absolutely no validity in the contemporary scene. Euthanasia is not a "good death". Euthanasia is when the doctor kills the patient.

Analyses of this issue also lay heavy emphasis on qualifying euthanasia and many dissect in detail what they see as active or passive euthanasia, as direct or indirect euthanasia, as voluntary, nonvoluntary or involuntary euthanasia, as assisted suicide. Grant that there is some value to these distinctions at times, but I also believe that their use, particularly detailed analyses of their differences, tends to cloud the issue. It would seem far more appropriate in the ongoing discussion to simply speak of euthanasia, and to continually call it what it truly is – *euthanasia is when the doctor kills the patient.*

The basic ethic of physicians down through the centuries has been consistent. Originated by a pagan physician, Hippocrates, 400 years before the time of Christ, that ethic was very clear. It was "primum non nocere", meaning "first do no harm". That ethic passed into the Christian era and guided the medical profession until recent decades. It has been increasingly violated in these past years, as some physicians have returned to the pre-Hippocratic ethic which gave to physicians two roles – the one of curing but also the one of killing.

Euthanasia was first practiced, on a large scale, in this century just prior to the Holocaust, which it prepared the way for. This should have taught us to never again repeat that horrible mistake. But time moves on, and we again are seeing a devaluation of human life.

The barrier was broken by the legalization of abortion which allowed licensed physicians to once again directly kill. Now the next barrier, that is, the killing of born people, is sorely threatened. Of course, we're told it

1

will only be done for the most serious cases, for those in the greatest pain, for those who are going to die anyway, etc. But this is a step that should not be taken. It is placing a price tag on human life – it is judging that human life has only a relative value, not an absolute, a sacred value.

When you place a price tag on human life, you have made a fatal move. The Nazis did that and promptly marked the price down. Modern day physicians in Holland did that and have been progressively marking the price tag down ever since. Abortion was first allowed for only those very difficult cases, but that was a price tag, and it has progressively been marked down. Let us not misunderstand for a moment – the slippery slope is a startling reality.

We must never forget William L. Shirer who interviewed a Nazi judge condemned to death at the trials of Nuremburg. The judge broke down and cried saying, "How could it have come to this?" Mr. Shirer responded, "Herr Judge, it came to this the first time you authorized the killing of an innocent life."

Proponents of euthanasia are quick to accuse doctors of not letting a patient die in peace. A typical picture is drawn of an old man tied down in bed, in constant pain, clearly dying. He has tubes in every natural body orifice and in several artificial ones. The doctor is keeping him alive, perhaps to obtain a larger fee, perhaps because the doctor does not want to admit that he is losing the battle for this man's life. This is echoed commonly in retirement communities where senior citizens can be heard to say, "I don't want you to keep me alive with all those tubes. I don't want those painful, expensive treatments. When my time comes, let me go." This is reflected in opinion polls which, with loaded wording, often return majority support for "assisted suicide". What most respondents mean by statements such as the above is that they should be allowed to die in peace. They don't really mean that they would favor a doctor coming to their bed, putting a needle in their vein and killing them with a lethal injection. We must, therefore, interpret such opinion polls with great caution, for when all of this is explained to people, polling results are rather dramatically different.

Your author has been treating people for fifty years. I vividly recall, as a medical student, having the professor come on to our ward holding up a vial of medicine and saying, "This is penicillin." We had two patients on that University Hospital ward who were inevitably going to die, as their conditions at that time were beyond cure. One was a severe osteomyelitis (bone infection) in a patient who was becoming septic. The other was a sub-acute bacterial endocarditis (heart infection). A choice had to be made, and, with the tiny amount of penicillin available then, the decision was made, curing one while we tragically watched the other disease take its course.

In the '50s and '60s we saw progressive, marvelous advances in treatment. Basic to this was the discovery and development of antibiotics, one after another, one more effective than the other, each new one treating a class of infections that the earlier ones could not touch. We were learning to conquer infectious diseases. This made so many other things possible – dramatic new surgical procedures, early ambulation of patients, the establishment of intensive care units for newborns and for adults. Along with these came other new drugs to treat blood pressure, heart failure, blood clots – and the list went on. It seemed, in those earlier years, that we could prevent death, and all physicians were more or less captivated by this. We had marvelous new tools to keep people alive, to cure diseases. We used them, but, in retrospect, we did not always know how or when to stop. Without question, in the decades of the '50s, '60s, even into the '70s, many of my colleagues kept people alive too long and did not let natural death occur, even when it was inevitable. Keeping people alive too long was expensive, emotionally draining on both patient and family and at times involved needless discomfort on the part of the patient – sometimes even prolonged pain.

Prior to the introduction of these new drugs and procedures, truly lifesaving treatments were limited. Only too often the physician's role was to comfort and to eliminate pain, as the patient progressed to an inevitable death. Next we went through the phase of keeping people alive, but not knowing when to "let go". That phase has largely passed. If anything, too often the pendulum has swung the other way. Today we are urged, sometimes prematurely, to write "do-not-resuscitate" orders. Patients are asked, when admitted to hospitals, to sign whether or not they want certain treatments.

One can debate the merits of withdrawing treatment, as there are goods and bads, and each case rests on its own individual merits. What is evident, however, is that the pro-euthanasia argument above, of that old man strapped in bed in pain, is no longer a valid argument, except perhaps in rare cases. Today, we, the medical profession, do let people die a natural death. Now, rather than over-treatment, we are being accused of under-treatment. With managed care coming upon us in an almost suffocating fashion, in some areas, over-treatment is but history, and my colleagues, in many cases, can only hope they will be allowed to give their patients adequate treatment.

Two words to remember are "biologically tenacious". These are people who some think ought to die, but who won't. Patients who are dying will go on to die. Dying patients are really not the ones whom the proponents of "assisted suicide" and euthanasia have in their sights. These people are going to die regardless of whether treatment is given or not. Rather, their true targets are those who are "biologically tenacious". Commonly, these people are not in pain. They are not on life support systems, but frequently are, at least by some judgments, a burden. These are people who have had strokes, who have progressive neurologic diseases such as multiple sclerosis and Lou Gehrig's Disease. These are people with quadriplegia, who have had head injuries, and others. These are people who someone thinks ought to die but who won't. These are the ones who are in the gunsights of those who would legalize euthanasia. They want them to get dead

The issue of pain control and of compassionate care are absolutely central to this debate. These are covered, in some detail, in Chapters VII and X. The Dutch euthanasia program is there for all to see. It is staring us right in the face. No one with a straight face can promote doctor-assisted suicide, which is euthanasia, without taking a long, considered look at what has happened and what is happening in Holland. It has been a proving ground to demonstrate what will happen in a society that legalizes euthanasia. Chapter VI gives us detail on Holland. Read it very carefully. What's happening there is clearly a prototype of what can and will, almost certainly, happen in other nations if euthanasia is legalized.

The chronologic logical progression is truly devastating. Read the German experience in Chapters II, III and IV. Then the Dutch and finally today's "assisted suicide". Each had and will have an inevitably more and more lethal progression.

Remember, heart-wrenching arguments will continue to be set before us . . . the so-called "hard cases". But if and when we legalize some form of euthanasia for those "hard cases", we will have opened the door. Then "the camel's nose" will truly be under the tent. Then we will have established that there can be a price tag on human life, a price tag that can and will be marked down. Then, once again, we will remember William L. Shirer's comment to that Nazi judge – "Herr Judge, it happened the first time you condemned an innocent man." And, for us, we must remember that it will happen the first time we allow, legally, a doctor to kill a patient.

CHAPTER II

LESSONS FROM HISTORY'S MOST CALAMITOUS EXPERIENCE

By Cathleen A. Cleaver and Edward Grant

As early as 1895, a widely-used German medical textbook made a claim for the "right to death." Immediately following World War I, the notion took deeper root in the German medical and legal professions, instigated largely by the 1920 publication of *Die Freigabe der Vernichtung lebensunwertens Leben* (Permitting the Destruction of Unworthy Life).

The connection of medical killing in Nazi Germany to contemporary debates regarding the legalization of assisted suicide and euthanasia has been a matter of great controversy. It is clear, however, that those closest to these events saw some connection. The condemnation of the "Nazi doctors" was universal and prompted great reflection on the question of ensuring that their actions never be repeated. As one step, the world's physicians reaffirmed the foundational ethical principle of their profession — that doctors must not kill their patients.

The acceptance by physicians of the notion that a "life not worthy to be lived" under the euthanasia program was a cornerstone of the horror that was to follow. Without the willingness of doctors to participate, the euthanasia program would not have occurred. This cornerstone principle persists today. The experience of the Netherlands establishes that the participation of physicians in killing their patients invariably rests upon, and propagates, the notion of life unworthy of life. The writings of pro-euthanasia philosophers James Rachels, Peter Singer, and John Harris confirm this fact[1]. While social and political conditions in Western democracies obviously differ from those of Nazi Germany, the consequences of legalizing physician-assisted suicide and euthanasia would be no less dire.

5

Proposals for Healing by Killing

In interbellum Germany, the medical and legal professions were influenced by proposals that patients in certain categories would benefit from hastened death. Thus, "the most humane, the most sophisticated, the most scientifically advanced medical community in the world" between 1920 and 1940 self-destructed while formulating and promoting ideas of physician-assisted death.[2] *Sterbehilfe*, "dying help," was advocated by the elite medical profession for the incurably sick and was considered to be *wohltat*, a merciful act.[3]

The influential publication by professors Karl Binding and Alfred Hoche, *Permitting the Destruction of Unworthy Life*, advocated *sterbehilfe* as a compassionate and humanitarian response for those who requested it, pursuant to a carefully controlled process. The text was "crucial" and "most important" in creating acceptance within the profession for direct medical killing, and for active participation in the euthanasia program that was to be instituted.[4]

Professor Binding was one of Germany's leading specialists in constitutional and criminal jurisprudence. Dr. Hoche was a psychiatrist. The jurist Binding queried, Should permissible taking of life be restricted to an individual's act of suicide as it is in current law, or should it be legally extended . . . to the killing of fellow human beings, and under what conditions?[5] He answered affirmatively for three groups of persons: (1) "those irretrievably lost as a result of illness or injury, who, fully understanding their situation, possess and have somehow expressed their urgent wish for release"; (2) "incurable idiots" from whom "here is no valid consent to be killed" but whose lives are "completely without purpose" and "a fearfully heavy burden both for their families and for society"; and (3) formerly competent patients who, due to trauma, "have become unconscious and who, if they should ever again rouse from their comatose state, would waken to nameless suffering."[6]

Hoche asked a somewhat different question, also answered affirmatively: "Is there human life which has so completely lost the attribute of legal value that its continuation has permanently lost all value both for the bearer of that life and for society?"[7]

Binding and Hoche explicitly condemned "mercy killings" that took place contrary to the will of the victims and emphasized the consent of the victims as a necessary condition for the killing of incurably ill people.[8] With regard to his first defined category, Binding stressed that the only people who may be candidates for permissible killings are those who are terminally ill and who "have either requested death or consented to dying."[9] Consent was of crucial importance to Binding: "*[E]very permitting of killing which requires violating the will to live of the actual or potential victim is ruled out.*"[10]

Hoche and Binding advocated providing sterbehilfe in a carefully controlled process, with evaluation by a three-person panel of professionals and the ability of the person to withdraw consent at any time.[11] They recommended that the initiative be made by the patient in the form of an "application for permission." The application would go to a government board composed of a physician, a psychiatrist, and a lawyer, and unanimity would be required in granting permission. The decree of permission would indicate that a "thorough investigation" had been undertaken, that the patient "seems beyond help," and that "there is no reason to doubt the sincerity of his consent."

Warnings

The Hoche and Binding monograph was much debated by the medical community in Germany after its publication. The legalization of medical killing was discussed and rejected at the 1921 *Karlsruhe Arztetag*, medical convention, and at the 1922 Dresden conference of the Society for Forensic Psychiatry.[12]

Critics from the medical community warned that compassionate release for the afflicted would only be the first step toward a new medical ethic of death. Dr. M. Beer wrote in his 1914 book, *Ein schoner Tod: Ein Wort zur Euthanasiefrage* (A Beautiful Death: A Word about the Question of Euthanasia), that physician aid-in-dying might be

> the first step, but whether it would be the last appears to me to be very doubtful. . . . Once respect for the sanctity of human life has been diminished by introducing voluntary mercy killing for the mentally-healthy incurably ill, and involuntary killing for the mentally ill, who is going to ensure that matters stop there?[13]

Critics of Hoche and Binding also despised the "utilitarian shopkeeper" mentality which appeared to inform the tract. Others worried about the inflationary, slippery-slope potentialities latent in the whole enterprise. A few had doubts regarding the inherent arbitrariness and perniciousness of value judgments regarding the value of human life.[14]

In a major response to Hoche and Binding, *Das Problem der Abkurzung "lebensunwerten" Lebens* (1925) (*The Problem of Cutting Short Life Unworthy of Living*), Dr. Ewald Meltzer hotly disputed the claim that

> people with mental handicaps had lost the last vestiges of human personality, stressing instead their capacity and will to enjoy life. [He argued that it is] "far more heroic to accept these beings to the best of one's abilities, to bring sunshine

into their lives, and therewith to serve humanity' than to kill them for utilitarian reasons . . . [A]ltruism was humanity's distinguishing feature, [and] asylums for handicapped people were not only valuable centers of scientific research, but also tangible manifestations of Christian charity.[15]

While Binding and Hoche turned out to be "the prophets of direct medical killing," their thesis remained a minority view within German psychiatry and medicine during the Weimar Republic.[16] The rise of the Nazis brought into power an ideology of eugenics that provided the environment for their thesis, with the willing cooperation of medical and academic leaders, to overcome the initial opposition.[17]

Eugenicist theories promoting sterilization and euthanasia were widely propagated in German society through education and other means. Among the most prominent means used was film. In his 1936 novel *Mission and Conscience* (and subsequent film entitled, "I Accuse"), Helmut Unger told a story of a young woman suffering from multiple sclerosis who believes that her life is no longer worth living and asks her physician husband to relieve her of her misery.

Several other pro-euthanasia films were produced during this period.[18] These films argued that a medical ethic of preserving life only caused unnecessary pain and misery. "We humans use science to prolong suffering, where we could use science to bring deliverance," one said.[19] Such an ethic, these films said, stemmed from an "exaggerated concern for humanity," combined with "a religion which is alienated from reality," and "the dictates of an outmoded law code," which ought to be abandoned.[20] Later, the key role of such images in leading to the acceptance of medical killing became apparent.[21]

Small Beginnings

The proposals of Hoche, Binding, and others in the German and international community in favor of physician aid-in-dying were put into practice in the 1930s. First, child euthanasia was permitted for disabled and "defective" infants and children. Soon thereafter, an adult program for an "easy death" for incurably sick and mentally ill Germans was instituted on grounds of compassion. Ultimately, the genocide that was the Final Solution grew out of these programs of medical killing.

This euthanasia program was motivated by a mixture of concerns, some statist and some humanitarian in nature. It is important to note, however, that racial and anti-Semitic sentiments played no role in the original design or implementation of this program. In fact, the German government "did not want to grant this philanthropic act to the Jews."[22] "[I]t is worth remembering that the engine which drove the early moral transformation of German medicine was not the ideology of racial discrimination, but medical economics."[23]

> [The] moral collapse of German medicine was not caused by anti-Semitism. Ironically, [Jews] did not deserve the 'benefit' of psychiatric euthanasia. [Nor was the collapse] caused by National Socialist pressure. . . . [T]he collapse did not begin with the hacks and quacks. It began at the top, with the heads of departments of academic medicine.[24]

Furthermore, it is critical to note that physicians were invited, not compelled or otherwise forced, to participate in this program.[25] "Doctors were never *ordered* to murder psychiatric patients and handicapped children. They were *empowered* to do so, and fulfilled their task without protest, often on their own initiative."[26]

Merciful Deaths for Children

The practice of euthanasia, as illustrated by two early cases, began with requests from individuals for physician-assisted death. In March 1937, a child was killed by his father because he was significantly mentally ill. When the father was put on trial for murder, the local health office came to his defense, influencing the court to grant him a nominal prison sentence instead of the death penalty asked for by the prosecutor.[27]

The next year, a man named Knauer wrote the German government asking that his blind and mentally retarded daughter, born without an arm and leg, be granted *gnadentod* (mercy death). The chancellor instructed his personal physician, Dr. Karl Brandt, to investigate, and, if the letter were true, to grant the request.[28] Brandt found "a child who was born blind, an idiot — at least it seemed to be an idiot — and it lacked one leg and part of one arm."[29] According to the testimony of Brandt, "The parents should not feel themselves incriminated at some later date as a result of this euthanasia — that the parents should not have the impression that they themselves were responsible for the death of this child."[30]

Both doctors and parents preferred to use euphemisms to allow for psychological defense mechanisms of rationalization and denial of what really was happening. After taking a poll of parental opinion, it was determined by the government that, although many supported *gnadentod* for their severely disabled children, "parents would prefer it if they were told that their child had succumbed to this or that illness."[31]

As many as 6,000 children were killed in this first phase of physician-assisted death in Germany.[32]

Merciful Deaths for Terminally Ill and Disabled Adults

The German government also received requests for a mercy death from adults with cancer and severe disabilities for a mercy death.[33] Numerous people, believing that they were acting with compassion, wished that their handicapped relatives could be "released from their suffering."[34]

In May 1939, an advisory group, the Committee for the Scientific Treatment of Severe and Genetically Determined Illness, was formed to determine whether and how a euthanasia program for children and adults would operate."[35] The adult project was housed in Berlin at number 4 Tiergartenstrasse, giving rise to its code name "T-4." In the beginning, there appeared to be a broad level of support for this throughout the country.[36]

Patients then began to be killed by lethal injection at various hospitals and other health care institutions. The T-4 doctors did not consider themselves to be killers, but ministers of medical treatment, although there was some concern that their actions be accorded some legitimate legal authority.[37]

In September 1939, the chancellor responded to pressure to provide legal immunity for the doctors engaged in *gnadentod* mercy killings, and he issued a memorandum stating:

> Reichsleiter [Philip] Bouhler and Dr. [Karl] Brandt, M.D. are charged with the responsibility of enlarging the authority of certain physicians, to be designated by name, in such a manner that persons who, according to human judgment, are incurable can, upon a more careful diagnosis of their condition of sickness, be accorded a mercy death.[38]

A law to legalize physician-assisted death explicitly was proposed in 1940. Like the version proposed in 1933, it provided:

> Anyone suffering from an incurable illness that leads to strong debilitation of either oneself or others can, upon explicit request of the patient and with the permission of a specifically appointed physician, receive dying help (*sterbehilfe*) from a physician.[39]

An additional clause provided further that those people who were mentally incompetent to decide for themselves to exercise this new "right" were entitled to have others make that decision for them on their behalf.

This law was never formally enacted because the decision was made "to keep the question of euthanasia a 'private matter' between doctors and their patients."[40] The German medical profession was determined to keep the practice in its hands alone. "The needle belongs in the hand of the doctor," said Viktor Brack, head of one euthanasia program, in 1939. Brandt agreed, stressing, "Gassings should only be done by physicians."[41]

Government legal authorities initially intended that the T-4 program's *sterbehilfe* would be lawful only for "those cases where physicians, upon their personal decisions, [can] relieve incurably ill patients from their suffering by administering a drug for mercy killing."[42] Within a short period of time, "a network of some thirty killing areas within existing institutions was set up."[43]

Morphine, scopolamine, and prussic acid (cyanide) injections were initially used for the T-4 project because they had more of a medical aura than gas. However, objections to use of carbon monoxide gas were soon overcome because, not only was it more efficient, but also, Brandt said, carbon monoxide was painless and "would be the most humane form of death."[44]

In January 1940, Brandt, Brack, and others conducted the first large-scale test of assisted death for incurable adults in a psychiatric hospital near Berlin.[45] It was a gassing process that "included a fake shower room with benches, the gas being inserted from the outside into water pipes with small holes through which the carbon monoxide could escape."[46]

What occurred in the adult program is exemplified by the hospital at Hadamar, one of the major T-4 institutions. Between January and August 1941, more than 10,000 mentally ill Germans were provided a "painless death" in the shower-room gas chambers at Hadamar.[47] Alfons Klein was an administrative supervisor at Hadamar.

> He testified at his war crimes trial that, from October 1940 until January 1941 [The Hadamar] Institution was maintained only for German mental patients. In January 1941, plans were made to kill mental patients and to burn the corpses. This method was carried on and used until August 1941, when it was discontinued.[48]

By 1941, word began to spread on involuntary killings. In August 1941, the psychiatric/physician-assisted death programs at Hadamar and the other T-4 hospitals were officially ordered to be discontinued. By this time, 80,000 to 100,000 people had been killed under the T-4 program.[49] At Hadamar, however, the program never ceased. Only the method of death changed. Another 3,500 were killed by lethal injection between August 1941 and August 1942.[50]

From Euthanasia to Genocide

World War II caused a change in emphasis and an acceleration of the killing process. Resources were scarce, and it was perceived that the armed forces had a greater claim to food, clothing, and medicine than did the sick, mentally ill, and social undesirables. The government accordingly took advantage of the distractions of the war to eliminate these "burdensome" people.

The original euthanasia project of killing those who were seriously ill was extended to killing virtually anyone whose death was desired under the new "14f13" program.[51] First, hospitalized Jews who had previously been denied a mercy death were given *sonderbehandlung*, "special treatment,"and killed along with Germans in the euthanasia program. Later it was ordered that Jews and other undesirables be transported from the concentration camps to the same killing centers used by the T-4 program.[52]

Overall, it is estimated that 5,000 were provided a "mercy" death in the child operation, 80,000 to 100,000 in the adult T-4 program, and 20,000 concentration camp inmates in the 14f13 project; "special treatment" against Jews in hospitals eliminated another 1,000.[53] Some estimate the total toll of physician-assisted death was 275,000.[54] Other estimates reach as high as 400,000 from the child euthanasia, T-4, *sonderbehandlung*, and 14f13 operations combined.[55] The true number of lives lost can never be known.[56]

Testimony from the Medical Case at Nuremberg

Perhaps the best evidence for concluding that society must refrain from permitting any degree of killing by physicians is the testimony of those who participated in these crimes, as well as those who investigated and prosecuted them. Throughout the Nuremberg trials, the defendants insisted that their actions were motivated by compassion and humanitarian concerns. Valentin Faltlhauser insisted that, for him, "the decisive motive was compassion."[57] Pediatrician Ernst Wentzler recalled, "I had the feeling that my activity was something positive, and that I had made a small contribution to human progress."[58]

Also prevalent was the sentiment that, as physicians, these defendants' actions ought not be scrutinized by lawyers and judges. Dr. Hermann Pfannmuller, medical director at the Elgfing-Haar asylum hospital, complained at his trial before the Nuremberg Tribunal, "I am a doctor confronted with a lawyer, and our points of view are completely divergent."[59]

Brandt, who had played a critical role in the original authorization of the euthanasia program, spoke most directly in defense of its legitimacy, arguing through his attorney that it was within the authority of the state to institute such a program. In the closing argument for his case, Brandt made the following personal statement:

> Do you think it was a pleasure for me to receive the order to permit euthanasia? For fifteen years I had toiled at the sickbed and every patient was to me like a brother. I worried about every sick child as if it had been my own. . . . I fully realize

the problem; it is as old as mankind, but it is not a crime against man nor humanity. It is pity for the incurable, literally. Here I cannot believe like a clergyman or think as a jurist. I am a doctor, and I see the law of nature as being the law of reason. In my heart there is a love of mankind, and so it is in my conscience. That is why I am a doctor! . . . Death can mean deliverance. Death is life — just as much as birth. It was never meant to be murder.[60]

Similar arguments were put forth by Klein and other defendants at the Hadamar trial. Klein insisted that it was only in extreme cases, such as those involving the final stages of tuberculosis, that patients were "helped along" and saved from an insufferable prolonged death. "Only those people died who were very close to death already," he said.[61] Other Hadamar defendants justified the killings as acts of "mercy" and "deliverance."[62]

The War Crimes tribunals invariably rejected these defenses. Nevertheless, they are indicative of the attitude that the defendants brought to their work in asylums and hospitals, an attitude which some specifically attributed to Hoche and Binding, and others to the general current of thought in German society. In the last of the major euthanasia trials, in 1986, the defendants repeated the refrain that they had killed "out of love and pity."[63] These latter-day restatements of the (failed) defenses offered by defendants of 40 years earlier suggests a level of sincerity inconsistent with the theory that these attempted justifications had been manufactured after the fact out of mere expediency. The perpetrators believed in the notion of "life unworthy of living" before, during, and after their horrendous crimes.

Those who investigated and prosecuted these crimes accepted the fact that these physicians had been corrupted, not merely by Nazi ideology, but first by acceptance of a fundamental change in attitude regarding the role of the physician toward the chronically sick.

U.S. Brigadier General Telford Taylor, chief of counsel for the prosecution at Nuremberg, described the prominent physicians who were tried and convicted of murder:

> The defendants . . . are charged with murder, tortures and other atrocities committed in the name of medical science . . . [They] did not kill in hot blood, nor for personal enrichment . . . they are not all perverts. They are not ignorant men. Most of them are trained physicians and some of them are distinguished scientists. The perverse thoughts and distorted concepts which brought about these savageries are not dead. They cannot be killed by force of arms. They must not

become a spreading cancer in the breast of humanity. They must be cut out and exposed.[64]

Dr. Leo Alexander noted the origin and persistence of such ideas in the wake of his experience as a medical expert at the Nuremberg medical trials:

> Whatever proportions these crimes finally assumed, it became evident to all who investigated them that they had started from small beginnings. The beginnings at first were merely a subtle shift in emphasis in the basic attitude of the physicians. It started with the acceptance of the attitude, basic in the euthanasia movement, that there is such a thing as a life not worthy to be lived.[65]

Justice Robert Jackson, chief of counsel for the United States at Nuremberg, issued a warning that should not be lost in the midst of arguments that American medicine will never be corrupted by the legalization of physician-assisted suicide:

> A freedom-loving people will find in the records of the war crimes trials instruction as to the roads which lead to such a regime and the subtle first steps that must be avoided.[66]

Conclusion

Frustrated with the ethic of "preserving every existence, no matter how worthless," Hoche in 1920 wrote, expectantly, "A new age will arrive — operating with a higher morality and with great sacrifice — which will actually give up the requirements of an exaggerated humanism and overvaluation of mere existence."[67] Euthanasia proponents of our day, too, seek with great zeal to usher in a new age. They speak, in words echoing from a distant era, about the cruelty of depriving those who are suffering from their desired means to peace and freedom from pain. Like Binding, they scold, "Not granting release by gentle death to the incurable who long for it: this is no longer sympathy, but rather its opposite."[68]

The early promoters of euthanasia appeared to be sincere in their belief in the virtues of merciful death. Today's promoters of physician-assisted suicide may also be sincere, but it is a sincerity born of an unpardonable carelessness. Unlike their predecessors, euthanasia proponents today have the benefit of the lesson of history, which has taught the true nature of physician-assisted killing as a false compassion and a perversion of mercy. History warns that the institution of assisted death gravely threatens to undermine the foundational ethic of the medical profession and the paramount principle of the equal dignity and inherent worth of every human person.

— By Cathleen A. Cleaver, Director of Legal Policy for the Family Research Council, Washington, D.C.; Edward R. Grant, Member of the Board of Directors of Americans United for Life and Counsel to the Subcommittee on Immigration and Claims, Committee on the Judiciary, U.S. House of Representatives; and Mark A. Rothe, an attorney in private practice in Virginia.

INTRODUCTION TO CHAPTER III

Editor's Note: This chapter and the next are reprinted from Frederic Werthem's *A Sign For Cain*, his classic work on violence. These had been published separately under the title of *The German Euthanasia Program* which is out of print. We are pleased to bring them back to you as part of this book. Because we print them intact, there will be some degree of repetition, particularly with the previous chapter. Both are rich, however, and we are the beneficiaries.

CHAPTER III
THE GERANIUM IN THE WINDOW

The Euthanasia Murders
By Frederic Wertham, M.D.

IF we want to understand violence as a whole, we cannot leave any of its major manifestations in a fog of half-knowledge. But this is exactly what has happened with an unprecedented occurrence of mass violence, the deliberate killing of large numbers of mental patients, for which psychiatrists were directly responsible. To both the general public and the psychiatric profession, the details and the background are still imperfectly known. This is not only a chapter in the history of violence; it is also a chapter in the history of psychiatry. Silence does not wipe it out, minimizing it does not expunge it. It must be faced. We must try to understand and resolve it.

It should be kept in mind at the outset that it is a great achievement of psychiatry to have brought about the scientific and humane treatment of mental patients after centuries of struggles against great obstacles. In this progress, as is universally acknowledged, German psychiatrists played a prominent part. And German public psychiatric hospitals had been among the best and most humane in the world.

In the latter part of 1939, four men, in the presence of a whole group of physicians and an expert chemist, were purposely killed (with carbon monoxide gas). They had done nothing wrong, had caused no disturbance, and were trusting and cooperative. They

The German Euthanasia Program

were ordinary mental patients of a state psychiatric hospital which was—or should have been—responsible for their welfare. This successful experiment led to the installation of gas chambers in a number of psychiatric hospitals (Grafeneck, Brandenburg, Hartheim, Sonnenstein, Hadamar, Bernburg).

Let us visualize a historical scene. Dr. Max de Crinis is professor of psychiatry at Berlin University and director of the psychiatric department of the Charité, one of the most famous hospitals of Europe. He is one of the top scientists and organizers of the mass destruction of mental patients. Dr. de Crinis visits the psychiatric institution Sonnenstein, near Dresden, to supervise the working of his organization. He wants to see how the plans are carried out. Sonnenstein is a state hospital with an old tradition of scientific psychiatry and humaneness. In the company of psychiatrists of the institution, Dr. de Crinis now inspects the latest installation, a shower-roomlike chamber. Through a small peephole in an adjoining room he watches twenty nude men being led into the chamber and the door closed. They are not disturbed patients, just quiet and cooperative ones. Carbon monoxide is released into the chamber. The men get weaker and weaker; they try frantically to breathe, totter, and finally drop down. Minutes later their suffering is over and they are all dead. This is a scene repeated many, many times throughout the program. A psychiatrist or staff physician turns on the gas, waits briefly, and then looks over the dead patients afterward, men, women, and children.

The mass killing of mental patients was a large project. It was organized as well as any modern community psychiatric project, and better than most. It began with a careful preparatory and planning stage. Then came the detailed working out of methods, the formation of agencies for transporting patients, their registration and similar tasks (there were three main agencies with impressive bureaucratic names), the installing of crematory furnaces at the psychiatric institutions, and finally the action. It all went like clockwork, the clock being the hourglass of death. The organization comprised a whole chain of mental hospitals and institutions, university professors of psychiatry, and directors and staff members of mental hospitals. Psychiatrists completely reversed their historical role and passed death sentences. It became

The Geranium in the Window

a matter of routine. These psychiatrists, without coercion, acted not figuratively but literally in line with the slogan of one of the most notorious concentration-camp commanders, Koch, the husband of Ilse Koch: "There are no sick men in my camp. They are either well or dead."

The whole undertaking went by different designations: "help for the dying," "mercy deaths," "mercy killings," "destruction of life devoid of value," "mercy action"—or, more briefly, the "action." They all became fused in the sonorous and misleading term "euthanasia." Strangely enough—or perhaps not so strangely —the name has persisted. We hear and read of the "euthanasia program," "euthanasia experiments," "euthanasia campaign," "euthanasia action," "euthanasia trials." In reality, these mass killings had nothing whatever to do with euthanasia. These were not mercy deaths but merciless murders. It was the merciless destruction of helpless people by those who were supposed to help them. There was nothing individual about it; it was a systematic, planned, massive killing operation. The whole proceeding was characterized by the complete absence of any compassion, mercy, or pity for the individual. What a physician does or should do with a special individual patient under special circumstances had absolutely nothing to do with those mass exterminations.

The greatest mistake we can make is to assume or believe that there was a morally, medically, or socially legitimate program and that all that was wrong was merely the excesses. There were no excesses. Rarely has a civil social action been planned, organized, and carried through with such precision. It was not a "good" death, as the term "euthanasia" implies (from *eu,* "well," and *thanatos,* "death"), but a bad death; not a euthanasia but what may be called a dysthanasia. Often it took up to five minutes of suffocation and suffering before the patients died. If we minimize the cruelty involved (or believe those who minimize it), these patients are betrayed a second time. It was often a slow, terrible death for them. For example, a male nurse of one of the state mental hospitals described the routine he saw through the peephole of the gas chamber: "One after the other the patients sagged and finally fell all over each other." Others have reported that the dead gassed victims were found with their lips pushed outward,

The German Euthanasia Program

the tip of the tongue stuck out between them, clearly showing that they had been gasping for breath.

The false term "euthanasia" was used by those who planned, organized, and carried out the action, and it is still being used now by those who do not know, or do not want to know, what really happened.

The ancients meant by euthanasia the art and discipline of dying in peace and dignity. The only legitimate medicosocial extension of this meaning is *help* toward that end, with special emphasis on relief from pain and suffering. Euthanasia in this sense is the mitigation and relief of pain and suffering of the death agony by medication or other medical means. For the physician, that means a careful diagnosis, prognosis, and consequent action in relation to a special clinical state. As in any other medical procedures, this may involve a certain risk which requires the physician's best responsible judgment in the individual case. Whatever problems this may represent, they have no relation whatsoever to this massacre of mental patients. To confuse the two means to confuse humanity with inhumanity.

When Dr. Hans Hoff, professor of psychiatry at the University of Vienna, begins his introduction to the recent book *Euthanasia and Destruction of Life Devoid of Value* like this: "As long as there are incurable, suffering and painfully dying people, the problem of euthanasia will be open to discussion," he is adding to the confusion and concealment, as does the author of this whitewashing book. These victims were not dying, they were not in pain, they were not suffering, and most of them were not incurable.

From the very beginning—that is, before the outbreak of war and before any written expression by Hitler—it was officially known to leading professors of psychiatry and directors of mental hospitals that under the designation of "euthanasia" a program was about to be carried through by them and with their help to kill mental patients in the whole of Germany. The object was "the destruction of life devoid of value." That definition was flexible enough for a summary proceeding of extermination of patients.

The term "euthanasia" was deliberately used to conceal the actual purpose of the project. But there is also a real confusion about the term that reaches into many quarters. In the *American*

The Geranium in the Window

College Dictionary, for example, "euthanasia" is defined as "the putting of a person to death painlessly." That is not euthanasia; it is homicide. If you "put a person to death," that is, deliberately kill him, you are committing murder. If it is done painlessly, it is still murder. Many murders, just like suicides, are committed without inflicting pain. In similar fashion, a widely used recent dictionary of psychological and psychoanalytical terms defines "euthanasia" as "the practice of ending life painlessly." Criminology is familiar with cases of mass murderers who made it a practice to do just that. For example, the man who over a considerable period of time lured good-looking young boys into the woods and put them to sleep, a sleep from which they never woke up. They were found, partly undressed, with peaceful expressions on their faces. That was not euthanasia, however; it was mass murder. The fact that such confused and confusing definitions are given in standard dictionaries is another documentation of my thesis that violence is much more solidly and insidiously set in our social thinking than is generally believed.

Just as the designation has been left in ambiguity, so also has the number of the victims. We read about "thousands" or "tens of thousands" or "almost a hundred thousand." But how many were there? One would think that this fact would be indispensable for understanding not only the history of violence but even that of psychiatry and of modern civilization in general. Yet in none of the publications, books, or news reports of recent years is a more-or-less-correct figure given. It is characteristic that without exception all the figures that are mentioned are far below the reality. The individual psychiatric hospitals were not so squeamish about the number of patients put to death while the program lasted. For example, in 1941 the psychiatric institution Hadamar celebrated the cremation of the ten thousandth mental patient in a special ceremony. Psychiatrists, nurses, attendants, and secretaries all participated. Everybody received a bottle of beer for the occasion.

We can get an idea of the proportional numbers involved by studying some partial but exact statistics referring to a special locality. From 1939 to 1945 the number of patients in the psychiatric hospitals of Berlin dropped to one-fourth of the original total. As the cause of this drop the official statistics give "evacuations." That

23

The German Euthanasia Program

is a euphemistic expression for the fact that three-fourths of the patients were transported to other institutions and killed. Sometimes patients slated for murder were not sent directly to the hospitals that had the proper installations, but went first temporarily to so-called intermediate institutions. In 1938 the psychiatric institutions of the province of Brandenburg had 16,295 mental patients of the city of Berlin. In 1945 only 2,379 were left. Almost 14,000 were destroyed. In the institution Berlin-Buch, of 2,500 patients, 500 survived; in the hospital of Kaufbeuren in Bavaria, of 2,000 patients, 200 were left. Many institutions, even big ones, *i.e.,* in Berlin, in Silesia, in Baden, in Saxony, in Austria, were closed entirely because all the patients had been liquidated.

In the special killing institutions the turnover was fast. The psychiatric institution Grafeneck normally had 100 beds. Early in the "action," within thirty-three days 594 patients died (*i.e.,* were killed). A while later, within forty-seven days 2,019 inmates were written off. Eventually the crematorium of Grafeneck smoked incessantly.

In 1939 about 300,000 mental patients (according to some figures it was 320,000) were in psychiatric hospitals, institutions, or clinics. In 1946 their number was 40,000. It was discussed during the project that 300,000 hospital beds would be made available by getting rid of mental patients.

The most reliable estimates of the number of psychiatric patients killed are at least 275,000. We have to realize particularly that the largest proportion of them were not "incurable," as is often lightly stated. Even if "euthanasia" is defined, as it falsely is, as "the killing of incurable mentally diseased persons," that is not at all what happened. According to the best established psychiatric knowledge, about 50 percent of them either would have improved to such an extent that they could have been discharged and lived a social life outside a hospital or would have gotten completely well.

Another misconception widely credited is that these patients had hereditary diseases. Even publications completely condemning the "euthanasia" action fall into this error. However, in the largest number of patients the hereditary factor played either no role at all or only the slightest (and that not well established scientifically). The whole number comprises both curable and incurable condi-

The Geranium in the Window

tions, psychopathic personalities, epileptics, encephalitics, neuro-logical cases, mental defectives of both severe and mild degree, arteriosclerotics, deaf-mutes, patients with all kinds of nervous diseases, handicapped patients who had lost a limb in the First World War and were in a state hospital, "cripples" of every de-scription, *et al.*

The indications became wider and wider and eventually in-cluded as criteria "superfluous people," the unfit, the unproductive, any "useless eaters," misfits, undesirables. The over-all picture is best understood as the identification and elimination of the weak.

A considerable percentage of the whole number were senile cases, including people who had no senile psychosis but were merely aged and infirm. Many of the old people included in the program were not in institutions but were living at home, in good health, with their families. A psychiatrist would go to these homes and give the aged people a cursory psychiatric examination. Of course, it is easy, if you confront a very old person with a lot of psychological questions, to make it appear that something is men-tally wrong with him. The psychiatrist would then suggest that such people be placed under guardianship and sent to an institu-tion for a while. From there they were quickly put into gas cham-bers. It is difficult to conceive that thousands of normal men and women would permit their parents or grandparents to be disposed of in this way without more protest, but that is what happened. As early as September, 1939, word had gotten about among the population in Berlin that inmates of homes for the aged had been exterminated and that it was planned to kill all aged invalids as quickly as possible.

During the first phase of the program, Jewish mental patients, old and young, were strictly spared and excluded. The reason given was that they did not deserve the "benefit" of psychiatric eutha-nasia. This lasted up to the second half of 1940. Eventually they were all rounded up, however, and by 1941, practically without exception, were exterminated.

Thousands of children were disposed of. A special agency ex-isted for them, consisting of a commission of three experts: one a psychiatrist and director of a state hospital, the other two promi-nent pediatricians. The children came from psychiatric hospitals,

The German Euthanasia Program

institutions for mental defectives, children's homes, university pediatric clinics, children's hospitals, pediatricians, *et al.* They were killed in both psychiatric institutions and pediatric clinics. Especially in the latter a number of woman physicians were actively involved in the murders. Among these children were those with mental diseases, mental defectives—even those with only slightly retarded intelligence—handicapped children, children with neurological conditions, and mongoloid children (even with minimal mental defects). Also in this number were children in training schools or reformatories. Admission to such child-care institutions occurs often on a social indication and not for any intrinsic personality difficulties of the child. One physician who killed such training-school boys and girls with intravenous injections of morphia stated in court to explain his actions: "I see today that it was not right. . . . I was always told that the responsibility lies with the professors from Berlin."

The chief of the mental institution Hadamar was responsible for the murder of "over a thousand patients." He personally opened the containers of gas and watched through the peephole the death agonies of the patients, including children. He stated: "I was of course torn this way and that. It reassured me to learn what eminent scientists partook in the action: Professor Carl Schneider, Professor Heyde, Professor Nitsche." This, of course, is not an excuse either legally or morally, but it is a causal factor which has to be taken into account. And when Dr. Karl Brandt, the medical chief of the euthanasia project, defended himself for his leading role in the action, he stated that he had asked for the "most critical" evaluation of who was mentally incurable. And he added: "Were not the regular professors of the universities with the program? Who could there be who was better qualified than they?"

These statements that leading psychiatrists supplied the rationalization for these cruelties and took a responsible part in them are true. We must ask ourselves what was the prehistory, in the previolence phase, of their ideas. Historically there were tendencies in psychiatry (and not only in German psychiatry) to pronounce value judgments not only on individuals, on medical grounds, but on whole groups, on medicosociological grounds. What was (and still is) widely regarded as scientific writing pre-

26

The Geranium in the Window

pared the way. Most influential was the book *The Release of the Destruction of Life Devoid of Value,* published in Leipzig in 1920. Its popularity is attested by the fact that two years later a second edition became necessary. The book advocated that the killing of "worthless people" be released from penalty and legally permitted. It was written by two prominent scientists, the jurist Karl Binding and the psychiatrist Alfred Hoche. The concept of "life devoid of value" or "life not worth living" was not a Nazi invention, as is often thought. It derives from this book.

Binding and Hoche speak of "absolutely worthless human beings"; they plead for "the killing of those who cannot be rescued and whose death is urgently necessary"; they refer to those who are below the level of beasts and who have "neither the will to live nor to die"; they write about those who are "mentally completely dead" and who "represent a foreign body in human society." It is noteworthy that among the arguments adduced for killing, the economic factor is stressed, namely, the cost of keeping these patients alive and caring for them. The psychiatrist author decries any show of sympathy in such cases, because it would be based on "erroneous thinking." The jurist author recognizes that errors in diagnosis and execution might be made. But he dismisses that like this: "Humanity loses so many members through error that one more or less really hardly makes any difference." In the beginning of the book we read about the feeling of "pity" for the patient. But in the bulk of the text the question of pity does not come up any more. It gets completely lost. Instead, both authors enlarge on the economic factor, the waste of money and labor in the care of the retarded. Both extol "heroism" and a "heroic attitude" which our time is supposed to have lost.

These ideas were expressed in 1920. Surely Hoche and Binding had not heard of Hitler at that time, nor did Hitler read this book. It is not without significance that at this time, when Hitler was just starting his career, the "life devoid of value" slogan was launched from a different source. Evidently there is such a thing as a spirit of the times which emanates from the depths of economic-historical processes.

This little book influenced—or at any rate crystallized—the thinking of a whole generation. Considering how violence-stimulat-

27

The German Euthanasia Program

ing the ideas in it are, it is significant that both authors were eminent men who played a role as intellectual leaders in a special historical period. This illustrates the proposition that violence does not usually come from the uncontrolled instincts of the under-educated, but frequently is a rationalized policy from above. Hoche was professor of psychiatry and director of the psychiatric clinic at Freiburg from 1902 to 1934. He made valuable contributions to neuropsychiatry. In his clinic a number of eminent specialists were trained—for example, Dr. Robert Wartenberg, who later became one of the outstanding and most popular teachers of neurology in California. Hoche's sound views on classification of mental diseases had considerable influence on American psychiatry, especially through Adolf Meyer, professor of psychiatry at Johns Hopkins.

Wherever his work touched on the social field, however, he had illiberal tendencies. For example, in a series of monographs which he edited, he published and gave wide currency to a book which tried to prove women intellectually inferior to men. In his work on forensic psychiatry, he exhibited a punitive, legalistic attitude with regard to sexual deviations. He was a reactionary opponent of psychoanalysis, not recognizing even Freud's well-established clinical observations. He regarded his book on the destruction of "life devoid of value" as one of his "more important" works.

The other author, Karl Binding, was professor of jurisprudence at the University of Leipzig. He was the chief representative of the retribution theory in criminal law. He combatted the idea that the protection of society is the purpose of punishment and that the personality of the criminal has to be taken into account. He taught that for every criminal deed there has to be full retribution. His son Rudolf G. Binding was also a jurist, and a recognized poet as well. When Romain Rolland in 1933 warned against Nazi violence and pleaded for humaneness, Rudolf G. Binding answered in a "Letter to the World." He advocated fanaticism on the part of everybody and called for "fanatics big and small, down to the children."

Another intellectual stream that contributed to the final massacre of mental patients was the exaggeration of the influence of heredity on mental disorders. The chief representative of this trend was Ernst Ruedin. Ruedin was professor of psychiatry at the univer-

The Geranium in the Window

sities of Basel, in Switzerland, and Munich. Some of his studies on heredity, and those of his pupils and associates (like Eugen Kahn, who later became professor of psychiatry at Yale), were undoubtedly valuable. This was widely recognized. He participated in the First International Congress for Mental Hygiene in Washington, D.C. But it was he who supplied the "scientific" reasons according to which mass sterilizations of all kinds of physically and mentally handicapped people took place. He was the chief architect of the compulsory sterilization law of 1933. This law was so vigorously formulated and interpreted (by Ruedin in 1934) that, for example, any young man with a harmless phimosis was forced to be sterilized. The summary official explanation for this was that he would be "incapable of achieving extraordinary performances in sport, in life, in war, or in overcoming dangers." The results of enforced castrations in the period from 1933 to 1945 are still quoted in current psychiatric literature without any critique of their inhumanity.

The compulsory sterilization law was the forerunner of the mass killing of psychiatric patients, which was organized and carried out with Ruedin's full knowledge. He expressly warned psychiatrists against the "excessive compassion and love of one's neighbor characteristic of the past centuries."

Against this theoretical-intellectual background, mental patients were sacrificed in psychiatric institutions and in the name of psychiatry. From its very inception the "euthanasia" program was guided in all important matters, including concrete details, by psychiatrists. The administrative sector was handled by bureaucrats who dealt merely with executive, management, and formal questions such as transport of patients, cremation, notification of relatives, and so on. Even the false death certificates were signed by psychiatrists. The psychiatrists made the decisions. For these physicians, as the physical chemist Professor Robert Havemann expressed it, denouncing the "euthanasia" murders, "the patient is no longer a human being needing help, but merely an object whose value is measured according to whether his life or his destruction is more expedient for the nation. The physicians took over the function of judge over life and death. . . . They made themselves into infallible gods." How matter-of-factly they considered this

The German Euthanasia Program

role is illustrated by the replies of the veteran director of one of the biggest and formerly most well-administered psychiatric hospitals during an interrogation:

Q. To how many children have you applied euthanasia in your hospital?

A. I couldn't tell you exactly. . . .

Q. To how many have you done that? 200? 500? 1,000?

A. For God's sake, I really don't remember how many there were. I really don't know whether there were a hundred or more.

Q. Do you know when euthanasia was practiced on the last child in your hospital?

A. I don't know exactly. But Dr. ———— says that until a short time before the arrival of the Americans [the American Army], children were still subjected to euthanasia.

Q. For how long have you practiced the euthanasia of children?

A. After so much time, I can't remember the dates exactly.

Q. When did the extermination of these children stop?

A. The extermination of these children never stopped until the end. I never received an order [to stop it].

Q. To how many adults did you apply euthanasia in your institution?

A. I don't know any more.

Q. How many adults have you submitted to euthanasia in your institution?

A. That didn't happen in my institution. I contented myself with transferring the patients [to other institutions where they were killed].

It has been stated that the psychiatrists were merely following a law or were being forced to obey an order. Again and again we read—as if it were a historical fact—of Hitler's secret order to exterminate those suffering from severe mental defect or disease. Those who hold the one-man theory of history (sometimes called the great-man theory of history), according to which important developments, for good or evil, are to be explained by the wish and will of one individual person, favor the illusion that such an order was the entire cause of the extermination of psychiatric patients. According to this view, everything was fine until that order was given and became fine again when the order was revoked. The reality was very different. There was no law and no such order. The tragedy is that the psychiatrists did not have to have an order.

The Geranium in the Window

They acted on their own. They were not carrying out a death sentence pronounced by somebody else. They were the legislators who laid down the rules for deciding who was to die; they were the administrators who worked out the procedures, provided the patients and places, and decided the methods of killing; they pronounced a sentence of life or death in every individual case; they were the executioners who carried the sentences out or—without being coerced to do so—surrendered their patients to be killed in other institutions; they supervised and often watched the slow deaths.

The evidence is very clear on this. The psychiatrists did not have to work in these hospitals; they did so voluntarily, were able to resign if they wished, and could refuse to do special tasks. For example, the psychiatrist Dr. F. Hoelzel was asked by the psychiatric director of the mental institution Eglfing-Haar to head a children's division in which many handicapped and disturbed children were killed (right up to 1945). He refused in a pathetic letter saying that his "temperament was not suited to this task," that he was "too soft."

Hitler gave no order to kill mental patients indiscriminately. As late as mid-1940 (when thousands of patients had been killed in psychiatric institutions), Minister of Justice Guertner wrote to Minister Hans Lammers: "The Fuehrer has declined to enact a law [for putting mental patients to death]." There was no legal sanction for it. All we have is one note, not on official stationery but on Hitler's own private paper, written in October, 1939, and predated September 1, 1939. Meetings of psychiatrists working out the "euthanasia" program had taken place long before that. Hitler's note is addressed to Philipp Bouhler, chief of Hitler's chancellery, and to Dr. Karl Brandt, Hitler's personal physician at the time and Reich Commissioner for Health. (Bouhler committed suicide; Dr. Brandt was sentenced to death and executed.) The note reads as follows:

Reichleader Bouhler and
Dr. Med. Brandt

are responsibly commissioned to extend the authority of physicians, to be designated by name, so that a mercy

31

The German Euthanasia Program
death may be granted to patients who according to human judgment are incurably ill according to the most critical evaluation of the state of their disease.

(Signed) Adolf Hitler

To kill patients (Hitler does not speak of mental patients), even if one were sure that they are incurable, is bad enough. But even if his wish, as the note clearly expresses it, had been executed, the number of victims would have been infinitely smaller and the whole proceeding could not have been carried out in the way in which it was carried out. Referring to this note, anyone could have refused to do what was later actually done. The note does not give the order to kill, but the *power* to kill. That is something very different. The physicians made use of this power extensively, ruthlessly, cruelly. The note is not a command but an assignment of authority and responsibility to a particular group of persons, namely, physicians, psychiatrists, and pediatricians. This assignment, far from ordering it, did not even give psychiatrists official permission to do what they did on a grand scale, *i.e.,* kill all kinds of people who were not at all incurable or even mentally ill, making no attempt even to examine them first. The assignment gives to the psychiatrist the widest leeway for "human judgment" and a "most critical evaluation." It certainly cannot be construed as an order to kill people with no serious disease or with no disease at all.

Even if the note was not meant to be taken literally, it was a formal concession to ethics and offered a loophole for contradiction or at least question. The psychiatrists in authority did not take advantage of this. Instead they initiated the most extreme measures and cloaked them in scientific terminology and academic respectability. No mental patients were killed without psychiatrists being involved. Without the scientific rationalization which they supplied from the very beginning and without their mobilization of their own psychiatric hospitals and facilities, the whole proceeding could not have taken the shape it did. They were responsible for their own judgments, their own decisions, their own acts. It helps us to understand the wide social ramifications of violence if we realize that from the highest echelons down, the psychiatrists acted spontaneously, without being forced.

The Geranium in the Window

A court in Coblenz probed this question most carefully in the case of three hospital psychiatrists who were charged with "aid to murder in an indefinite number of cases": "They have taken this task upon themselves voluntarily, just as altogether the collaboration in the 'action' was voluntary throughout." This is borne out by a letter from Himmler, chief of the SS, in response to an inquiry by a high judge: "What happens in the place in question [a psychiatric institution] is carried out by a commission of physicians. . . . The SS furnish only help in vehicles, cars, etc. The medical specialist, expert and responsible, is the one who gives the orders." In this connection the statement of Dr. Hans Hefelmann, an agronomist who was a highly placed bureaucrat in the "euthanasia" program, is significant. He made it in the abortive "euthanasia" trial at Limburg in 1964: "No doctor was ever ordered to participate in the euthanasia program; they came of their own volition." Other evidence confirms this.

What psychiatrists did made even members of the Nazi Party weep. When patients were transferred from their regular institution to one where they were to be killed, they were usually told that it was only a regular normal transfer from one hospital to another or that it was a change to a better place. Sometimes a glimpse of the truth would become known to patients, and scenes worthy of Callot or Goya would follow. Here is such a (true) scene. In the sleepy little town of Absberg, two large autobuses (belonging to a central transport agency of the "euthanasia" program) are parked on the street near an institution where there are several hundred mental patients. Some time before, twenty-five patients had been fetched by such a bus. Of these twenty-five, twenty-four "died" and one woman patient returned. The other patients in the institution learned what had happened, as did the inhabitants of the town. As the patients leave the institution to enter the buses, they are afraid, they refuse and remonstrate. Force is used by the personnel, and each patient is shoved violently into a bus. A large group of bystanders has assembled. They are so moved that they break into tears. The whole operation is presided over by an experienced psychiatrist from the big state hospital Erlangen. Among those spectators who cried openly at this pitiful spectacle were—as

The German Euthanasia Program

the official Nazi report states—"even members of the Nazi Party." There is no mention anywhere that doctors had any tears in their eyes.

To place causal responsibility on the physician does not in any way diminish the responsibility of the high and low Nazi officials and bureaucrats involved. But by the same token, placing full responsibility on these officials does not in the slightest diminish the role of the psychiatrist in the slaughter. In order to get the proper focus, we must think in terms of causal factors. If it takes two to plan and commit deliberate murder, that does not mean that only one is guilty. Even if the psychiatrists had been under orders, which they were not, it is noteworthy that their complete mobilization for killing patients went as speedily and as smoothly as the military mobilization of soldiers to fight the enemy.

Two "extenuating" circumstances, often claimed, have to be seriously weighed. One is that the psychiatrists did not know; the other is that very few were involved. In the very beginning, some psychiatrists may not have known what happened to their patients when they were transferred en masse in buses to other, unnamed institutions. But it is preposterous to assume that this ignorance could last after tens of thousands had been killed. The claim that only a few psychiatrists were involved is equally invalid. The lowest estimate is that there were "perhaps fifty" who participated. Even if this were a correct number (which it is not), among them were some of the most renowned and distinguished academic and hospital figures. Actually, the extent of the operation makes it inevitable that there were many more involved in Germany and in Austria, perhaps three or four times that many (not to speak of the many psychiatric nurses acting under the instructions of psychiatrists). Of course, the degree of participation varied. For example, in the internationally famous hospital of Gütersloh, the director and his staff did not "select" patients for annihilation. But they delivered the patients, without resistance or protest, to the guards and escorts who drove up for them in trucks. That is participating in murder too.

In July, 1939, several months before Hitler's note was written, a conference took place in Berlin in which the program to kill mental patients in the whole of Germany was outlined in concrete,

The Geranium in the Window

final form. Present and ready to participate were the regular professors of psychiatry and chairmen of the departments of psychiatry of the leading universities and medical schools of Germany: Berlin, Heidelberg, Bonn, Würzburg. Historians of medicine and sociologists will have a lot of work to do to explain this. So far they have not stated the problem or even noted the fact. At a conference in Dresden in March, 1940, Professor de Crinis, of Berlin University, talked over the program with the chief psychiatrists of large public mental hospitals (state hospitals). The classification of mental disorders on which devoted physicians in all countries had worked for centuries was reduced to a simple formula: patients "not worthy to live" and patients "worthy to be helped." There was no opposition on the part of the physicians, every one of whom held a responsible position in the state-hospital system. Questions of ethics or the juridical aspects were not even mentioned. The only questions raised by the participants at the conference were how the project could be carried through most "practically and cheaply." For example, the transfer of patients from their original institution to one where they were to be killed was called "impractical" because it meant "wasting of gasoline." Mass graves, to be leveled later, were recommended as being an economical procedure.

For several years during the time of the program, psychiatrists held meetings every three months in Heidelberg under the chairmanship of the professor of psychiatry at the University of Heidelberg. At these conferences the ways to conduct the extermination action were studied, and suitable measures were suggested to assure its efficacy.

The whole project is a model of the most bureaucratic mass murder in history. It functioned as follows. In the preparatory meetings the chief psychiatric experts of the project worked out the criteria by which patients should be selected. Questionnaires were prepared with questions as to diagnosis, duration of stay in the institution, and so on. In October, 1939, the first questionnaires went out to state hospitals and other public and private institutions where mental patients, epileptics, the mentally retarded, and other handicapped persons were taken care of. Copies of each filled-out questionnaire were sent to four psychiatric experts, who indicated with a + or — their opinion about whether the patient

35

The German Euthanasia Program

was to live or die. (No expert gave an opinion on questionnaires filled out for patients in his own institution, but only on those of other institutions. Therefore he had no personal knowledge whatsoever of the patients.) This typical correspondence shows that the psychiatric experts worked very hard.

Letter from the "euthanasia" central office in Berlin to Member of the Commission of Experts, dated November 25, 1940:

Enclosed I am sending you 300 report sheets [questionnaires] from the institution Lüneburg with the request for your expert opinion.
(Signed)

Answering letter from the Member of the Commission of Experts to the central office in Berlin, dated November 29, 1940:

Enclosed I am sending you the 107th batch of report sheets, namely, 300 sheets complete with my expert opinion.
(Signed)

This rapid selection and certification of death candidates is not a record or by any means exceptional. The same expert formed his opinion on 2,190 questionnaires in two weeks and on 258 in two days.

The questionnaires with expert opinions indicated by the + or the — were then sent to a chief expert, who passed the final judgment. Beginning in January, 1940, the patients marked for death were transferred, directly or via intermediate stations, to the six psychiatric institutions in which gas chambers had been installed for the program. In these lethal institutions the patients were dealt with summarily and quickly, as this typical letter shows, from the social-welfare association Swabia to the director of the state hospital Kaufbeuren:

I have the honor to inform you that the female patients transferred from your hospital on November 8, 1940, all died in the month of November in the institutions Grafeneck, Bernburg, Sonnenstein, and Hartheim.
(Signed)

In some institutions, like Hartheim in Austria, things went so fast sometimes that it took only four hours from the time a patient was admitted till he left "through the chimney."

36

The Geranium in the Window

The backbone of the whole project was the experts. It was their decision which sealed the fate of every victim. Who were these men? That is the most remarkable part of the story—and the most important one for the future of violence and, I believe, of mankind. They were not nonentities or outsiders. Most of them had all the hallmarks of civic and scientific respectability. They were not Nazi puppets, but had made their careers and reputations as psychiatrists long before Hitler came to power. Among them were more than twelve full professors at universities. Most of their names read like a roster of prominent psychiatrists. They have made valuable contributions to scientific psychiatry. They are still quoted in international psychiatric literature, which testifies to their scientific stature. The bibliography of their papers, monographs, and books—not to mention their graduate and postgraduate lectures and their editorial work on leading psychiatric journals—would fill a whole brochure. We must make ourselves familiar with the caliber of these men if we want to comprehend the full meaning of this historical occurrence.

Dr. Max de Crinis was professor of psychiatry at the University of Berlin and director of the psychiatric department of the famous Charité Hospital. He was originally chief physician at the psychiatric clinic at the University of Graz. Those who knew him personally describe him as a "charming Austrian." He has many scientific studies to his credit, on alcoholism, epilepsy, war neuroses, pathology of the central nervous system (brain edema and brain swelling), etc. He was especially interested in the bodily concomitants of mental disorders—for instance, malfunction of the liver. Textbooks, including recent ones, refer to some of his scientific work as authoritative. In 1944, he published an interesting book on the somatic foundations of emotions which is still quoted in the scientific literature today. It is not easy to understand—but is important to know—how such a man could deliberately and personally, from his own department in the university hospital, send a thirteen-year-old boy afflicted with mongolism, with only minor mental impairment, to one of the murder institutions—the children's division of Goerden—to be killed. In 1945, when his car could not get through the Russian encirclement of Berlin, Dr. de

The German Euthanasia Program

Crinis committed suicide with a government-supplied capsule of cyanide.

One of the most distinguished (and most unexpected) members of the team of experts which was the heart of the whole killing operation was Werner Villinger, who at the time was professor of psychiatry at the University of Breslau. Prior to that he was head of the department of child psychiatry at Tuebingen and then psychiatric director at Bethel, a world-famous institution for epileptics and mentally and physically disabled persons founded in 1867. From 1946 to 1956 he was professor of psychiatry at the University of Marburg. His clinical research on the outbreak of an acute psychosis after the commitment of a violent crime became well known. He wrote especially on the psychological and social difficulties of children and youths, on child guidance, group therapy, juvenile delinquency, and similar subjects. He has been decorated by the West German government. In 1950 he was invited to participate in the White House Conference on Children and Youth and did so.

His name alone, quite apart from his activity in it, gave a great boost to the "euthanasia" project. For his name suggested to others, especially younger psychiatrists, that there could be nothing wrong with the "action." It is difficult to understand how a man with concern for youths could not only consent to but actively participate in projects of killing them, but we may find some slight hints in his previous writings. Two years before Hitler came to power, Villinger advocated the sterilization of patients with hereditary diseases. Writing about the "limits of educability," he stated that "the deepest roots of what we call temperament and character are deep in the inherited constitution." Contrary to our modern point of view, he regarded the chances for the rehabilitation of juvenile delinquents with definite emotional difficulties as very poor.

During the preparation of the "euthanasia" trial in Limburg, Dr. Villinger was questioned by the prosecutor in three sessions. At about the same period, it became publicly known that he was implicated in the "euthanasia" murders in a leading, active role. He went to the mountains near Innsbruck and committed suicide. An attempt was made later to make this appear an accident, but there is no doubt about what happened.

38

The Geranium in the Window

To find Dr. Carl Schneider as a leading member of a wholesale murder project is also unexpected. For twelve years he was professor of psychiatry at the University of Heidelberg. As such he held the same important position as Emil Kraepelin a generation before. And Kraepelin was the founder of modern clinical psychiatry. In a recent textbook, Schneider's scientific work is referred to eleven times. In some of the most recent publications on the course of mental diseases and on the effect of tranquilizers, his clinical subdivisions are taken as a basis. He made clinical investigations of mental disorders in organic brain diseases and in pernicious anemia. He wrote on abnormal personalities in relation to diminished legal responsibility. Since experimental psychoses are currently much investigated, it is of interest that more than thirty years ago he induced an experimental psychosis in himself with mescaline. He described it in his monograph on hallucinations. One of his monographs deals with "The Treatment and Prevention of Mental Disorders." He studied epilepsy and expressed modern views about it, and his research on that subject is still quoted. He wrote two books on schizophrenia. The first, *The Psychology of Schizophrenia,* is considered a landmark of this type of clinical study. Originally more interested in subtle psychological analyses, he stressed more and more the hereditary factor.

Carl Schneider was very active in all phases of the program. He served as expert for the processing of death questionnaires, participated in the frequent conferences, and regularly instructed younger psychiatrists in the methods and procedures of the project. Perhaps the most extraordinary part of this story is that before going to Heidelberg, he, like Werner Villinger, had held the highly respected position of chief physician at the universally recognized institution Bethel. Ten years later, when he was professor at Heidelberg, he appeared with an SS commission at Bethel, went over the questionnaires, ordered the personnel to present patients to him, and personally selected the candidates for extermination. When, after the defeat of the Nazi regime, Dr. Schneider was to be put on trial, he committed suicide.

Another psychiatrist with an international reputation is Professor Paul Nitsche. He was successively director of several state hospitals, including the tradition-rich Sonnenstein in Saxony, which

The German Euthanasia Program

was the first psychiatric state hospital in Germany. In the authoritative *Handbook of Psychiatry* (1925–1932), he wrote the section on "Therapy of Mental Diseases," based on his own vast experience. He was one of the editors of the German *Journal for Mental Hygiene*. He wrote understandingly on modern psychotherapeutic measures in mental hospitals. He was interested in psychoses in prisoners (prison psychoses), and his book on the subject appeared in the best American monograph series on nervous and mental diseases. In the killing project he held a top position. He functioned as a representative of Dr. Brandt, the "leader" of the medical sector (as opposed to the strictly administrative bureau). He did his work of organizing and selecting death candidates so well that during the project he was advanced from expert to chief expert.

Nitsche presents perhaps the most remarkable psychological enigma. Colleagues of his who knew him well and who condemn him for his "euthanasia" work nevertheless say of him that he was "an exceptionally good psychiatrist, especially kind to his patients and concerned about them day and night." So can a false fanatical social orientation play havoc with a man's character. Here we come up against a contradiction which plays a great role in modern violence: the contrast in the same individual between the private, intimate, spontaneous personality and the corporate, public, official personality.

After the Nazi regime ended, Dr. Nitsche was tried in Dresden for the murder of mental patients and was sentenced to death. In 1947 he was executed.

Perhaps the greatest break with the humane traditions of psychiatry is connected with the name of Dr. Werner Heyde. Heyde was professor of psychiatry at the University of Würzburg and director of the psychiatric clinic there. Few places in the world can look back on such a long history of successful care of mental patients. The clinic grew out of a division of a general hospital where mental patients were admitted and kindly treated as early as the last decades of the sixteenth century. It is interesting that exactly contemporary with the extant case histories of this hospital are the descriptions by Cervantes in *Don Quixote* (first chapter of the second part) of the mental institution in Seville (around 1600).

The Geranium in the Window

Cervantes' stories of the inmates show that this institution (*casa de los locos*) was humanely administered. In other words, in two geographically widely separated and different localities, Seville and Würzburg, pioneer work was done that long ago in treating the mentally afflicted as human beings and as medical patients. It is certainly a problem for the historian of culture, as it is for the student of violence, that in the same place where mental patients were treated most humanely in 1583, they were doomed to be killed in 1940. In the later nineteenth and in the twentieth century, the Würzburg psychiatric clinic played a prominent role in scientific research. A number of outstanding psychiatrists got their training there. The first intelligence test was devised there in 1888. One of the earliest clinical observations and descriptions of what was later called schizophrenia came from that clinic.

Dr. Heyde's reputation as a scientic psychiatrist was excellent. He worked for several years in the clinic, became director of the out-patient department, and began his teaching there in 1932.

One of Heyde's predecessors as head of the Würzburg clinic, Conrad Rieger, who studied especially the history of psychiatry, wrote, almost prophetically, in his autobiography in 1929 (ten years before the start of the extermination program): "Whether it is deliberate or through negligence, it is wrong to kill human beings and to deprive them of care. On the contrary, we must care for them and protect them, well and humanely. This care and protection is needed in the same measure for the so-called curable and the so-called incurable." We do not know whether Heyde ever read this statement, which he so completely reversed. Heyde was a key figure in the program. When carbon monoxide was suggested as a method for killing, this proposal had to be submitted first to him for evaluation. He approved the method and directed the idea into the proper administrative channels for its practical realization. He was the head of one of the agencies of the project, the Reich Society for Mental Institutions (state hospitals). In his office the data from these institutions were collected and the last word pronounced about the patients to be sent to the special extermination hospitals. He played the leading role in the preparatory and organizing conferences (before Hitler's private note), helped in working out the questionnaires, functioned as chief expert, and

41

The German Euthanasia Program

selected the younger psychiatrists for the program and instructed them in their task.

From the beginning, he personally inspected the death institutions and the installation of the gas chambers, to make sure that everything functioned expeditiously. In addition, far from being told what to do, he gave lectures before high officials in the Nazi ministries to promote and explain the weeding out of those "not worthy to live." For example, on April 23, 1941, in the Department of Justice, he gave a lecture on "The Euthanasia Program" before high officials, judges, and prosecutors. The most important person present was the president of the highest court, the Reich Court, Judge Erwin Bumke. Bumke had been appointed to his office in 1929, during the democratic Weimar Republic. He raised no objection to the mass killing after this lecture, and the doom—the legal doom—of the mental patients was sealed. Psychiatry and law had met in the spirit of violence.

After the collapse of the Nazi regime, Heyde was arrested, but he escaped from custody. A warrant for his arrest ("Wanted for Murder . . ."), with his picture on it, was sent out. It said that he was probably working as a physician. For twelve years he lived a charmed existence under a different name. He was employed by a state insurance agency, again as chief expert. He did a great deal of work for courts. During this time his wife was receiving a widow's pension, and from money earned in his new career she bought a beautiful house on Lake Starnberg, near Munich. Many private persons—judges, prosecutors, physicians, university professors, and high state officials—knew his real identity. There was a certain solidarity in protecting this secret of violence. When his identity did come out, almost by accident, he surrendered to the authorities. His trial at Limburg was delayed for four years for preliminary investigation. He made another attempt to escape, which failed. When he was left unguarded in his cell five days before the trial was due to start, he committed suicide.

This trial, which would have been the most important "euthanasia" trial, delayed overlong, never took place. One day before Dr. Heyde's suicide, his codefendant, Dr. Friedrich Tillman, who from 1934 to 1945 was director of orphanages in Cologne and who has been called a "bookkeeper of death," jumped or was

The Geranium in the Window

pushed from a tenth-story window. Another defendant, Dr. Gerhard Bohne, escaped from jail to South America. And the fourth defendant, Dr. Hefelmann, was declared not able to stand trial because of illness. The widely held belief that there was great pressure against this trial's taking place seems to be not without foundation.

Among other outstanding professors of psychiatry who were involved in the program were the following:

Dr. Berthold Kihn was the professor of psychiatry at the famous University of Jena, where Hegel, Fichte, Schiller, and Haeckel taught, where Karl Marx got his doctor's degree and the composer Schumann an honorary doctorate. He contributed chapters to several authoritative textbooks—for example, on neurosyphilis, on peripheral nerves, and on disorders of old age. He did research on the microscopic study of brain tissues. Kihn not only was busy making the death crosses on questionnaires, but also personally supervised the selection of patients for extermination in various institutions. He and Dr. Carl Schneider were among the charter members of one of the main project agencies.

Dr. Friedrich Mauz was professor of psychiatry at Koenigsberg from 1939 to 1945 and has held the same position at the University of Münster since 1953. A good deal of his scientific work became generally acknowledged: his studies on hysteria and epilepsy, with interesting clinical observations; on psychoses in juveniles; on the physical constitution in mental disorders. From him comes the term "schizophrenic catastrophe," for the most severe progressive types of the disease. In 1948 he participated as one of three official delegates from Germany at an international mental hygiene meeting in London. At that congress, the World Federation for Mental Health was founded, its purpose being the "furthering of good human relations."

Dr. Mauz excused himself later, without any condemnation of the "euthanasia" project, by saying that his invitation to a "euthanasia" conference in Berlin was "harmlessly formulated" and that as late as the autumn of 1940 (when tens of thousands of patients from all over Germany had been killed and whole hospitals closed because all the patients had been evacuated to death institutions), he, who held a responsible and administrative position in psy-

The German Euthanasia Program

chiatry, did not know anything about any "carrying through of the euthanasia program."

This list is far from complete.

In the whole "euthanasia" matter the universities, including the psychiatric and pediatric departments, wrapped themselves in silence. How easy it would have been (and riskless) to refuse, had anyone been so minded, is shown by the case of Gottfried Ewald, professor of psychiatry in Göttingen. He was invited to a conference at the central office in Berlin under the chairmanship of Heyde and was asked to join the program. He refused and left the conference. He remained unmolested and had no disadvantage on account of his complete refusal.

There is an interesting sidelight on his exceptional behavior. Among those whom the experts marked on the questionnaires or report sheets as "unworthy to live," and who were consequently killed, were veterans who had lost an arm or leg in the war. The records are clear about that. For example, among a group of male patients transferred from the state hospital Rottenmuenster to a death institution was one whose "euthanasia" questionnaire said: "Receives war pension. Handicapped for work through loss of an arm." Professor Ewald had lost his left arm in World War I and referred to it occasionally in his lectures. Maybe that made it easier for him to identify with the victims.

A young German psychiatrist of much lower rank, Dr. Theo Lang, made a serious attempt to stem the whole program. He was at that time in Germany and later became chief physician of the institution Herisau in Switzerland. On January 20, 1941, he obtained an interview with Dr. M. H. Goering at the German Institute for Psychological Research and Psychotherapy. His plan was to get Dr. Goering to sign a declaration against the extermination of mental patients. When he tried to tell Dr. Goering the whole story of the program, which at that time had been going on for more than a year, he found that Dr. Goering knew all about it and confirmed its truth. However, he refused to sign the declaration, and so nothing came of this *démarche*.

In taking this step—and for this reason his name should not be forgotten—Dr. Lang showed extraordinary courage. In going to Dr. Goering, he knew that he was approaching the very seats of

The Geranium in the Window

Nazi power, both political and psychiatric. Dr. Goering was a cousin of Marshal Hermann Goering, with whom he was in personal contact. And his close collaborator and coeditor on the Nazi-coordinated *Journal for Psychotherapy* for several years was Dr. C. G. Jung. Dr. Jung, in the words of the then State Secretary for Health, Dr. Conti, "represented German psychiatry under the Nazis." So Dr. Lang could not reach any higher with his plea for mercy and decency.

In addition to the professors of psychiatry, the experts included directors of large and well-known state hospitals from different parts of Germany, like Buch, near Berlin, and Eglfing, near Munich. They were also busy making the death crosses on the questionnaires and helping in other ways. These experts were not new appointees of the Nazi regime, but had had long and honorable careers. They were by no means products of Nazism, but were parallel phenomena. Their thinking was similar: the attacking of a social problem by violence. However well disguised by high-sounding terms like "eugenics" and "euthanasia," the problem was essentially economic and sociopolitical, namely, the cost of care for the temporarily "unproductive" and the prosperity and glory of the nation.

It is important to keep in mind that among those in responsible positions and most actively engaged in the killing were psychiatrists of ability. For example, Dr. Valentin Falthauser, director of a state hospital, was sentenced to three years in prison for practices that contributed to the death of three hundred hospital inmates. He was coauthor of an important book *Home Care in Psychiatry and Allied Fields,* which contains ideas which are still of great actuality for current community psychiatry.

The special agency for child "euthanasia," the Reich Commission for the Scientific Registration of Hereditary and Constitutional Severe Disorders, had as its most prominent expert Dr. Werner Catel, who was subsequently professor of pediatrics at the University of Kiel until the sixties. This was a commission of experts, psychiatric and pediatric, that decided—entirely on its own—which children should be killed as being mentally below par or handicapped or physically malformed. Dr. Catel still defends and advocates his type of "euthanasia" today—for instance, in his

45

The German Euthanasia Program

book *Borderline Situations of Life* (1962). It is a noteworthy fact for the recognition of the violence content of a democratic society that the head of a child-killing organization with thousands of victims should become the professor of pediatrics and head of a pediatric clinic at a renowned university.

The children slated for death were sent to special "children's divisions," first Goerden, then Eichberg, Idstein, Steinhof (near Vienna), and Eglfing. They were killed mostly by increasing doses of Luminal or other drugs either spoon-fed as medicine or mixed with their food. Their dying lasted for days, sometimes for weeks. In actual practice, the indications for killing eventually became wider and wider. Included were children who had "badly modeled ears," who were bed wetters, or who were perfectly healthy but designated as "difficult to educate." The children coming under the authority of the Reich Commission were originally mostly infants. The age was then increased from three years to seventeen years. Later, in 1944 and 1945, the work of the commission also included adults.

A further method of "child euthanasia" was deliberately and literally starving children to death in the "children's divisions." This happened to very many children. In most instances, these deaths were recorded as normal or natural deaths. But many people knew about the fact itself. As early as autumn 1939, a student of psychology, later a public-school teacher, Ludwig Lehner, was permitted with other visitors to go through the state hospital Eglfing-Haar. He went there as part of his studies in psychology. In the children's ward were some twenty-five half-starved children ranging in age from one to five years. The director of the institution, Dr. Pfannmueller, explained the routine. We don't do it, he said, with poisons or injections. "Our method is much simpler and more natural." With these words, the fat and smiling doctor lifted an emaciated, whimpering child from his little bed, holding him up like a dead rabbit. He went on to explain that food is not withdrawn all at once, but the rations are gradually decreased. "With this child," he added, "it will take another two or three days."

Surely this is a scene worse than Dante. But the punishment was anything but Dantesque. In 1948, Dr. Pfannmueller was specifically charged in court with having ordered the killing of at least 120

The Geranium in the Window

children and having killed some himself. It was testified that he had personally killed some of the children with injections. He was sentenced to six years in jail, of which he served two years. That makes about six days per killed child.

How great the professional moral confusion can become is evident from this sidelight. Professor Julius Hallervorden, a well-known neuropathologist, after whom a special brain disease is named (Hallervorden-Spatz disease), asked the central office of the program to send him the brains of "euthanasia" victims for his microscopic studies. While the victims were still alive, he gave instructions about how the brains should be removed, preserved, and shipped to him. Altogether he got from the psychiatric death institutions no less than six hundred brains of adults and children. It evidently did not occur to him, or to anybody else, that this of course involved him seriously in the whole proceeding. An American professor of psychiatry at a well-known medical school told a national magazine that there was no ethical problem involved here and that Dr. Hallervorden "merely took advantage of an opportunity."

By the middle of 1941, at least four of the death hospitals in Germany and Austria not only killed patients but became regular murder schools: Grafeneck, in Brandenburg; Hadamar, near Limburg; Sonnenstein, in Saxony; and Hartheim, near Linz. They gave a comprehensive course in lethal institutional psychiatry. Personnel were trained in the methods of assembly-line killing. They were taught the mass-killing techniques, "gassing," cremation, and so on. It was called basic training in "mercy killing." The "material" for all this training was mental hospital patients. On them the methods were tried out and tested before they were applied later to Jewish and other civilian populations of the occupied countries. Technical experience first gained with killing psychiatric patients was utilized later for the destruction of millions. The psychiatric murders came first. It is a revealing detail that a man named Gomerski, who was engaged in mass killing in the death camps of Sobibor and Treblinka, was nicknamed the Doctor because of his "euthanasia" training in the psychiatric hospital Hadamar.

The method of taking out gold fillings and gold teeth from victims was first tried, worked out, and routinely used on the mental-

47

The German Euthanasia Program

hospital patients killed. Only after that was it practiced on concentration-camp inmates. The patients had to open their mouths
and a number was stamped on their chests. From this number the
personnel knew which patients had gold teeth, so that they could
be removed later. The first human-derived ingots of gold for the
Reichsbank were made from the gold from the mouths of these
mental patients. According to sworn testimony, several grams of
gold meant several thousand people killed. In Berlin there was a
special office, the Central Accounting Office, to keep track of the
proceeds from killed mental patients. How to take gold teeth from
the dead was taught as a special skill. For example, in the institution Hadamar, a man named Loeding had learned this "break-
ing of teeth," as it was called. Later he was transferred for this
purpose to the institution Eichberg. All this was done in the name
of euthanasia. Later it was applied to millions of people.

Toward the end of 1941 the gas chambers in the death institutions were dismantled, transported to the east, and there freshly
erected for their new tasks in concentration camps. Meanwhile the
killing of mental patients went on with other methods, with injections, for instance. "Only" a few thousand were now being killed
each month.

Some of the same psychiatrists who selected patients in hospitals went to concentration camps and selected death candidates
there. Himmler had the idea of having the inmates of these camps
examined "to comb out" those to be eliminated. He needed suitable physicians. So the central bureau of the "euthanasia" program
supplied him with "experienced psychiatrists." In practice, this
worked out as follows. In 1941 a commission of five went to the
concentration camp Dachau to select prisoners to be transferred to
Mauthausen to be killed. All five men were psychiatrists, and their
chief was a professor of psychiatry of the University of Berlin. As
they sat at tables put up between two barracks, the inmates had
to file past while the doctors looked at their records. The criteria
for selection were set by two chief experts in psychiatry. They
consisted in (*a*) ability to work and (*b*) political reports. Several
hundred of the so-selected prisoners were sent to Mauthausen and
destroyed there.

The director of the state hospital Eichberg, Dr. Fritz Mennecke,

The Geranium in the Window

who went to concentration camps as expert to select death candidates, was asked in court about the two types of cases he had judged interchangeably, the mental patients on medical grounds and the camp prisoners on political grounds. "One cannot separate them," he answered. "They were not subdivided and neatly separated from each other."

The typical case of Dr. Adolf Wahlmann, psychiatrist at the state hospital Hadamar, shows how easy the change was for some psychiatrists from killing mental patients to killing foreign civilians. He was not a Nazi and not a sadist. He had had a good medical education in the universities of Giessen, Marburg, Erlangen, and Kiel and had worked for years in responsible psychiatric posts in different institutions. In the Hadamar institution, thousands of mental patients were killed. In 1944 shipments of Polish and Russian men, women, and children from other institutions and work camps in occupied territories were sent to Hadamar. They were killed by lethal injections which he prescribed, exactly as he had done before with mental patients.

There is a persistent myth about the whole "euthanasia" project which serves to ease the conscience of the civilized world. It is entirely false. According to this myth, Hitler stopped the program after about a year (when "only" some 70,000 patients had been killed) because of protests and pressure from the churches and the public. The "euthanasia" killing was *not* stopped. It went on until 1945, to the end of the Hitler regime—and in some places, *e.g.,* Bavaria, even a few days longer. There is no evidence that it was stopped; all the evidence is that it continued. It did not end; it merely changed its outer form. It did not even get less cruel but in many cases was more cruel. The killing was not done as before, in the form of conspicuous big actions, but was carried out in a more cautious form and at a slower pace. From 1941 on, instead of the gas chambers (which had been transferred), other methods were used. Without any formal procedure and without any norm, it was carried out by individual institutions and individual doctors. They selected, decided, and acted. The end effect was the same. The methods employed were deliberate withdrawal of food, poisoning, or in many cases a combination of both. The poisoning was done by injections of overdoses of drugs. Patients

49

screaming from hunger were not unusual. If it got too bad, they were given injections which quieted them, made them apathetic, or killed them. This was called euthanasia too. "Euthanasia" by starvation. Such methods had the advantage of more discretion: patients who were destroyed in this way could be more easily counted as "natural deaths." It was the occupation by the Allied armies both in the north and in the south which freed the remaining patients from the psychiatrists.

Examples of continued general "mercy killings" after their alleged end in the summer of 1941 exist for every year thereafter, until 1945. At the end of 1942, at a conference of state officials and the directors of state hospitals, there was a discussion of the "excellent" method of making the "useless eaters" (*i.e.,* patients) die by "slow starvation." A hospital employee has reported that in 1940 she worked in one of the death-dealing hospitals; then she was transferred to another, where the patients were not killed with gas but with injections and overdoses of drugs; she worked there until 1943; she was sent to a third hospital, where the same procedures were used until the overthrow of the regime in 1945. The chief male nurse of one mental hospital described the progression. In 1940 the program started when mental patients were gassed to death and then burned. In 1941 the gassing was discontinued. Beginning in 1942 the patients were killed with lethal doses of morphine, scopolamine, Veronal, and chloral. In 1944 foreign slave laborers from the camp were also admitted to the hospital and killed in the same way. This account is entirely uncontested testimony and is typical for the whole project. In 1944 patients were still being transported from their hospitals to "special institutions" (to be killed) under the pretext that it was a regular routine transfer from one hospital to another.

With respect to children, the legend of the 1941 ending of "mercy deaths" does not have even a semblance of truth. The child-killing agency functioned openly and efficiently till the collapse of the regime in 1945. Nobody has claimed that it ended before. Under its auspices, the mass murder of children continued routinely all over Germany and Austria. In Vienna, for example— the golden Viennese heart notwithstanding—children were killed in the children's division of the famous institution Steinhof and the

The Geranium in the Window

municipal children's institution Spiegelgrund until the end of the war. Professor I. A. Caruso, now well known for his book *Existential Psychology,* who as a young psychologist witnessed some of this himself, says of the Reich Commission that its "murderous activity" was "massive." It was also, as one writer put it, unbelievably cruel.

As for the Hitler "order" for the alleged termination of the project, no document existed, not even a private note as at the outset of the "action." What happened was that in the late summer of 1941 in his General Headquarters, in a conversation with his physician, Dr. Karl Brandt, Hitler asked for the "provisional cessation of the euthanasia action on a large scale." This was purely verbal and was not written. It was an organizational change. It was clearly foreshadowed in a previous statement by Gestapo chief Himmler that there were "faults in the practical procedures." (The killing with the gas installations was too conspicuous.) Soon after Hitler's talk with Dr. Brandt, the chief expert, Professor Heyde, made it very plain in a written communication that the change was merely a "technical matter." Indeed, the gas chambers were moved, but the killing in the mental institutions in Germany continued with other methods.

As for the resistance of the churches, the fact that the killing did continue shows that it was not so strong or so persistent as to be effective. It was not enough. Dr. Karl Brandt stated that it was Hitler's opinion (which proved right) that resistance to the "euthanasia" killings on the part of the churches would under the circumstances not play a great role. The efforts were sporadic, isolated, and fragmentary. At certain levels the attitude was for a long time so passive and ambiguous that a top bureaucrat in the mercy killings, Hans Hefelmann, could state truthfully in court in Limburg that it had been his understanding that the church "was willing to tolerate such killings [at the time] under certain conditions."

What clergymen did was sixfold. They first protested about the transfer and eventual killing of patients in institutions under their jurisdiction. They wrote to the government and submitted evidence. They protested against the project from the pulpit. In some, but not all, institutions where religious sisters worked as nurses, the clergy made the further work of the sisters dependent on the as-

The German Euthanasia Program

surance that they did not *have* to "participate" in any way in any part of the project. They reported instances to local juridical authorities as punishable crimes. (This was of no effect, because all complaints relating to the "action" were forwarded to Berlin and disregarded.) Finally we know of at least one occasion when a prominent clergyman achieved a long personal interview with one of the officials of the program and pleaded with him. A highly respected pastor, Fritz von Bodelschwingh, the chief of the Bethel institution, invited Dr. Karl Brandt to visit Bethel. Dr. Brandt accepted and the two men conferred for three hours.

It was a memorable event. Dr. Karl Brandt was a complex personality. He knew Dr. Albert Schweitzer well, was impressed with his theory of "reverence for life" and interested in his philanthropic work. As a young doctor he had planned to work with him as an assistant in Lambaréné in Africa. The only reason why that did not come about was that Brandt was born in Alsace and the French would have called him up in Lambaréné for military service. We can speculate that his whole career might have been different—in fact, might have taken just the opposite direction—if social preparation for war and violence had not prevented it. From what Pastor Bodelschwingh related later of their talk, Dr. Brandt tried to explain that the "euthanasia" project was necessary to save the nation. Bodelschwingh's position was that nobody has the right to be inhuman to his fellowmen. It seems that as a result of this discussion the liquidation of the "not worthy to live" inmates of Bethel was at least postponed and it may have helped many to escape this fate.

On March 8, 1941, the Catholic bishop Clemens von Galen of Münster, in Westphalia, spoke from the pulpit against the "euthanasia" action. He said: "These unfortunate patients must die because according to the judgment of some doctor or the expert opinion of some commission they have become 'unworthy to live' and because according to these experts they belong to the category of 'unproductive' citizens. Who, then, from now on could still have confidence in a physician?" This sermon helped to inform the public further but it had no lasting effect. For it was only a one-shot condemnation, not followed up by the bishop, not reinforced by higher dignitaries of the church, and not backed by Rome. (Von

The Geranium in the Window

Galen died a Cardinal in 1946.) The forces of destruction and propaganda had become so entrenched that the public could no longer do anything about it anyhow.

Why, then, in 1941 was the program changed in methods, speed, and conspicuousness? From the historical context of events and opinions, it is abundantly clear why Hitler interfered. He was concerned, and rightly so, with military morale. Would the spirit of the troops hold out to see the war through? It was late summer of 1941. Soldiers were learning that at home Germans were killing Germans. They were afraid that the wounded with head injuries would be sent to the gas chambers—and this might well happen to them. So the gas chambers were conspicuously dismantled. Moreover, going home on leave they might find that a grandparent or other aged relative had disappeared. Morale became affected, so it was more or less officially given out that the program was stopped. In reality it continued, but less blatantly than before.

In June, 1945, the American Military Government, through its Public Health and Security officers, investigated the psychiatric institution Eglfing-Haar, on the outskirts of Munich. In this hospital, some 300 children, from six months to sixteen years old, and about 2,000 adult patients had been killed on a thoroughly organized basis. This went on until the American occupation. Some of the adult patients had not been killed in the place itself but had been sent to an institution at Linz for killing and cremation. There were, at the very minimum, thirty such hospitals in Germany with "special departments" for destroying patients.

In Eglfing-Haar, which had had an excellent reputation as a psychiatric hospital, there was a children's division with a capacity of about 150 children called the *Kinderhaus*. This division had a "special department" with twenty-five beds and cribs for the children about to be exterminated. In June, 1945, it was still occupied by twenty children. They were saved by the American Army. In the children's "special department" there was a small room. It was bare except for a small white-tiled table. At the window was a geranium plant which was always carefully watered. Four or five times a month a psychiatrist and a nurse took a child to this little room. A little while later they came out, alone.

The killing of children was carried out by different methods.

53

The German Euthanasia Program

One was overdoses of Luminal given either by injection or as a powder sprinkled over food. Another method was injection of a drug called modiscope, a combination of morphine, dionine, and scopolamine. Some children were given iodine injections with the result that they died in convulsions. Among the victims were retarded children who could have been taught and have led well-adjusted lives. Some were emotionally disturbed children who could not play well with other children and were regarded as "antisocial." The brains of the murdered children were sent to a psychiatric research institution for scientific microscopic studies.

The killing of adults was done almost entirely by deliberate starvation. The patients were given only vegetables and water until they died. They never got bread or meat or anything else. In this "special department," until the American Military Government took over, no patient got any treatment whatsoever, mental or physical. If he cut himself, he was not bandaged and was allowed to bleed. The selection of the patients to be put into this "special department" was largely in the hands of the staff psychiatrists and was a matter of routine. One criterion for selection was the length of stay in the institution. The whole procedure was known to all the hospital personnel.

We are still in the postviolence phase of the "euthanasia" murders. That is perhaps one of the darkest spots of the story. For the whole action has been minimized and left in a cloud of obfuscation, concealment, and social forgetfulness. We read about errors where there really was precision, about excesses where there were regular procedures, about dictates where there was all too ready compliance, about "misunderstood humaneness" where there was routine inhumanity. This happens not only in popular literature, but also in the writings of leading professional men.

To some extent, the courts have contributed to the confusion, which in its turn breeds indifference. For what were identical or very similar crimes, the sentences were of the greatest imaginable variety. A very few of those involved were sentenced to death and either executed or given death sentences which were commuted to life imprisonment and then reduced further; many were pardoned; in a number of cases, the courts decided that there was no case and no occasion for a trial; many were acquitted or received rela-

The Geranium in the Window

tively short jail sentences; most remained entirely unmolested by the law and continued their professional or academic careers.

In some instances, the courts have made general statements about the project which tend to minimize its wrongfulness. For example, a court in Munich decided that "the extermination of mental patients was not murder, but manslaughter." In this summary form, which has been quoted in newspapers and magazines, the statement might give some people the dangerous idea that killing one person may be murder, but killing many is just manslaughter.

The reasons the courts have given for leniency or acquittal are revealing:

A court in Cologne, in acquitting one of the physicians, spoke of the victims, the patients, as "burned-out human husks." In another court opinion, the patients are called "poor, miserable creatures."

The director of a psychiatric hospital which served as an "intermediate institution" had accepted patients and then sent them on to death institutions with full knowledge of their eventual fate. The court gave as one reason for his acquittal that his role "does not represent an acceleration of the process of destruction, but a delay, and therefore a gain of time [for the patients]."

The director of a state hospital was acquitted on the ground that the many patients in whose death he was instrumental would have perished anyhow.

In a number of cases, the courts acted as if to kill or not to kill was a metaphysical question, like "to be or not to be." They quote the "ethics of Plato and Seneca" or speak of a "tragic conflict of duties" (acquittal in both cases).

Classic is the judgment of a Frankfurt court about a psychiatrist who not only killed many patients—adults and children—personally, but also watched their death agonies through the peep window of the gas chambers. "We deal," said the court, "with a certain human weakness which does not as yet deserve moral condemnation."

In the same way, in the case of a pediatric clinic in Hamburg where many children were deliberately killed ruthlessly, a medical organization proclaimed that the "actions of the inculpated female and male physicians in the years from 1941 to 1943 under the

The German Euthanasia Program

circumstances obtaining at that time did not represent any serious moral transgressions." And a medical journal stated that no professional action was indicated (such as depriving the physicians of their right to practice or to work in hospitals) because after the murders "their work in their profession was beyond reproach."

There has been—and still is—a great reluctance to face the whole "euthanasia" project as what it really was. We are concerned that the truth may damage the image of psychiatry (and pediatrics). But is not the substance more important than the image? A successful effort has been made to hush the whole thing up, in a cloud of silence, distortion, abstract speculations about life and death, irrelevant discussions of the duties of the doctor, and wholly irrelevant misuse of the term "euthanasia." In a recent book by a physician, Professor de Crinis is praised as a "courageous and energetic physician." The book *Euthanasia and Destruction of Life Devoid of Value* (1965), by the present professor of forensic and social psychiatry at the University of Marburg, speaks of the "comparatively few [*sic*] mental patients" killed. (This book is highly recommended in a recent number of an American psychiatric journal.)

In 1950 the then director of the state hospital Bernburg wrote an article in a scientific psychiatric journal in celebration of the seventy-fifth anniversary of that institution's beginning. In Bernburg more than 60,000 people had been murdered, the psychiatric director during that time having been a willing tool of the "euthanasia" project. The anniversary article speaks three times of the "reputation of the institution" as if that were the main point and calls the period of the mass killing an "episode and a step backwards" comparable to the (unavoidable) disruption of the service in the First World War.

This is violence unresolved. The psychiatric profession, to the limited extent that it has spoken at all, claims that the "euthanasia" murders were "ordered" by the Nazis. The record shows that is not true. But even supposing it were true, can we accept the position that if a political party "orders" the psychiatric profession to murder most of its patients, it is justified in doing so?

A recent trial in Munich throws light on several aspects of both the action phase and the postviolence phase of the "euthanasia"

The Geranium in the Window

murders. What was established there was entirely typical. Tried for participation in murder were fourteen nurses of the psychiatric state hospital Obrawalde-Meseritz in which at least 8,000 mental patients (including children) were killed. This killing went on until 1945. The nurses gave lethal doses of drugs to the patients. The staff psychiatrists, male and female, selected the patients who were to be killed, prescribed the lethal doses, and ordered the killing. Once, in the beginning, when a nurse refused to give a deadly dose of Veronal (barbital) to a woman patient, the female chief psychiatrist gave her a "big bawling out." The defense of the nurses was that "we had to bow to the orders of the physicians." Routinely two or three patients were killed every day; in 1945 the number was increased to four a day. On the weekends there was no killing; it was a matter of "never on Sunday." After the end of the Nazi regime, most of the fourteen nurses continued in their regular professional work in hospitals as before. Three were working as nurses in hospitals at the time of the trial. All fourteen were acquitted. It was a triumph for the Goddess of Violence.

We are not dealing here with just the behavior of individual practitioners or professors or with just an accident in the practice of a science. What confront us are crucial problems in the relation of science and medicine to society and politics, of the value of human life versus national and social policy. We can learn what Dr. Richard Madden, a physician and social historian of "fanaticisms," wrote a hundred years ago, that behind all the veneer there is still "a great deal of savagery in the heart's core of civilization."

CHAPTER IV
LOOKING AT POTATOES FROM BELOW

– Administrative Mass Killings –
By Frederic Wertham, M.D.

THE administrative mass killings of the Nazi era constitute something new in the rich history of human violence. Even individuals
cannot be completely understood henceforth without a realization
of how easy it is for a civilized society to revert to a state of
brutality. No single deed or event of this period is entirely new.
But the total process is new. It manifests itself on different levels—
political, psychological, military, institutional, and economic. It is
a mixture of brutality, efficiency, and cynicism about human life.
From the concentration camp Flossenbürg in Bavaria, where
thousands of resistance fighters were killed, a guard wrote in a
letter to a friend that there was always room there for more people
"because from time to time some of them look at the potatoes
from below."

The methods by which the victims were killed, their numbers,
the deliberate inclusion of women and children, and the way it
was rationalized, accepted, defended, and perpetrated are all a
recent dimension of violence. We cannot visualize this from big
generalizations, but only from typical examples. In the neighbor-
hood of the Serbian town of Kragujevac, partisans clashed with
a Nazi detachment. As a result, 6,000 inhabitants of the town
were later seized as hostages and killed. Among them was a whole

The German Euthanasia Program

secondary school, of which the director, the teacher, and every single pupil were killed. Such acts were not committed, as is sometimes stated, by "outsiders of society." They were carried out by ordinary people and planned, ordered, and acknowledged by the highest authorities.

The mass killing in concentration camps cannot be subsumed under any of the old categories. It is not bestial, because even the most predatory animals do not exterminate their own species. It is not barbaric, because barbarians did not have such organized, planned, and advanced techniques for killing people and processing them into such commercial products as fertilizers. It is not medieval —it is indeed very twentieth century. It is not strictly a national matter, for the perpetrators had no difficulty in finding collaborators —even very active ones—in other countries. It is not a past, historical episode, because it is still largely unresolved legally, politically, psychologically and educationally. It is not a unique occurrence, because there is no certainty whatsoever that it will not be repeated when similar circumstances arise. It is not an unforeseeable natural catastrophe, because it was long foreshadowed. It is not the work of madmen, for many of the perpetrators and organizers led (both before and after the killings) normal, average bourgeois, working-class, professional, aristocratic, or intellectual lives. The term "genocide" covers only a part of it (although a very large one), because the earliest part was strictly political: Germans killing Germans. It was not a disorderly orgy of primitive violence but a mass action lasting years and carried out with pedantic orderliness.

A mass murderer used to be a man who killed maybe four or five or, say, even ten or fifteen people. Those were what are called the good old days. Now mass killing involves hundreds or thousands. These numbers are so large that we can hardly imagine them. It is also difficult to apply to them the categories of individual responsibility, guilt, being an accessory, punishment, and so on.

The people killed in concentration camps included political prisoners, Jews (the largest number), gypsies (the most completely exterminated group), Slavs, prisoners of war, and undesirable civilians. It has been estimated that 7,500,000 people were con-

"Looking at Potatoes from Below"

fined in concentration camps, of whom a bare 500,000 survived, many with serious mental and physical aftereffects. The number of Jews killed in concentration camps and outside is estimated at between 5,000,000 and 6,000,000.

By 1945 there were in Germany, Austria, and occupied countries more than a thousand concentration camps. Among them were:

Auschwitz (Oswiecim)

Belsen, near Hanover

Belzec, in Poland, the first big concentration camp where gas chambers were installed; about 600,000 victims died there

Birkenau, the poetically named camp (meaning "meadow of white birches") which was part of the Auschwitz complex

Buchenwald, near Weimar

Chelmo (Kulmhof)

Dachau, one of the earliest central camps

Dora, in Thuringia, part of the Buchenwald complex, where V-2 rockets were manufactured by slave labor and many died in the subterranean installations

Flossenbürg, in Bavaria, for political prisoners and others

Gross-Rosen

Hellerberg, near Dresden; nearly all its inmates were later killed in Auschwitz

Hohnstein, in Saxony, which was regarded as one of the worst

Janowska, in Poland

Maidanek, also in Poland, one of the largest annihilation camps

Mauthausen, in Austria

Natzweiler, in Alsace

Neuengamme, near Hamburg

Oranienburg, near Berlin, one of the earliest camps

Ravensbrück, in Brandenburg, a central death camp for women, where 92,000 women and children were killed

Sachsenhausen

Sobibor, in Poland

Theresienstadt (Terezin), in Czechoslovakia

Treblinka, in Poland

From Belzec, Sobibor, and Treblinka, the authorities, after deduc-

The German Euthanasia Program

tion of all overhead and expenses for transportation, derived pure profits of $44,500,000, profits which were handled by the Reichsbank and the Ministry of Economics. (This sum included profits from the victims' possessions, clothes, gold teeth, hair, and so on.)

We are apt to think of concentration camps as enclosures with a few buildings surrounded by barbed-wire fences and located in isolated places. In reality there were barracks, many buildings, big industrial installations, factories, railway stations with regular railway services, ramps, roads, connections with nearby towns and villages, big warehouses for products from the corpses and the victims' belongings, installations for torture and killing, research institutes, distribution centers, gas ovens, crematory furnaces, human-bone-milling plants, well-appointed kennels for hundreds of police dogs, agricultural fields, gardens for the officials, and so on. Some of the bigger camps were in reality groups or systems of different camps. All this in the aggregate covered large territories and involved wide communications. These ramifications alone show the absurdity of the claim and belief that the population knew nothing about them. These camps were going concerns. Thousands of people in the camps and in the population had working contacts with them.

The methods used in these camps were varied. They included, among others, shooting, hanging, poisoning, torturing, beating to death, "extermination by labor" (*i.e.,* working to death), starvation, carbolic acid injections into the heart, burning alive, wounding and leaving to die in mass graves with others already dead, vivisection, stomping, drowning, electrocution, locking as a group in a bunker and throwing hand grenades into it, freezing either in icy water or from standing naked in snow, clubbing or kicking to death, and keeping people packed in upright position in a cell with only standing room till they died.

One aspect of the administrative mass murders was the inclusion of children. This fact has been generally soft-pedaled and is little mentioned. This is an omission which helps to obscure the whole picture of the violence of our time. It has been estimated that about 1,500,000 children were killed, ranging in age from infancy up. Many of them were asphyxiated in gas ovens. The expression generally used for this procedure was "chasing the children up the chimney." The child phase of the mass murders had three features. First, it was carried out with the greatest brutality. Second, it was not a matter of individual excesses (although that happened often too, especially for sexual reasons), but was part of the routine and a regular constituent of policy and strategy mapped out at the desks of highly placed officials. Third, it was not carried out only by the SS; ordinary people did it as well. Painful medical experiments that often led to death were also carried out on children by physicians.

We can best imagine the official attitude toward children in concentration camps from a scene that took place in Auschwitz. A young child walked straight through the camp. Around his neck was hung on a string a placard with his name on it in big letters. That was most unusual. Why was he wearing it? He was the son of the camp leader, Aumeier, on his way to visit his father, and if he had not worn such a sign he might have been snatched up on the spot and tossed into one of the gas ovens.

There are two kinds of violence. The first is violence accompanied by emotion: feelings of hate, sadism, sex, and other passions. The second variety has very little to do with the personal passions of men. It is impersonal and bureaucratic, and those who order, commission, and organize it as well as those who execute it have extremely little feeling for their victims, be it sympathy or hate. They are executioners or slaughterers. Among the Nazi killings were many examples of sadistic cruelty, but the bulk of these killings was on a different plane. It is difficult to grasp intellectually or emotionally the reality of these assembly-line executions. We must string together a whole list of adjectives to convey their nature: collective, bureaucratic, administrative, methodical, planned, calculated, organized, systematic, stereotyped, routine, efficient, impersonal, purposeful. As one survivor expressed it, it was "a fantastically well-organized, spick-and-span hell."

The roots of this callousness go back to the time before the Nazi regime. The twenties in Central Europe was not only the time of the Weimar Republic of Thomas Mann and the Bauhaus, but also very much the time of the rise of extreme reactionary groups, who made no secret of their intentions. The portents of this previolence phase were not recognized then and are not even

The German Euthanasia Program

fully recognized historically now. If we do not follow all the sources of the administrative mass murders, it means that these victims have not only suffered, they have suffered in vain. Odd Nansen, the son of the explorer and Nobel Peace Prize winner Fridtjof Nansen, was an inmate of the Sachsenhausen concentration camp. He described his experiences and observations and wrote: "The worst crime you can commit today against yourself and society is to forget what happened and sink back into indifference. It was the indifference of mankind that let it take place."

We should not regard the Nazi mass killings of civilians in isolation. Many extensive massacres and exterminations have occurred in the past: the Crusades (a million victims); the Massacre of St. Bartholomew's Day; the Inquisition (a quarter of a million); the burning of witches (at least 20,000); the subjection of colonies in South America (more than 15,000,000); the island of Haiti (14,000 survivors out of 1,000,000 inhabitants after thirty-five years of colonization); the extermination of the Indians in Argentina and Uruguay, the island of Mauritius (the work slaves died so fast that 1,200 had to be imported annually); Java (the Dutch East India Company extorted in twelve years $830,000,000 from the slave labor of 5,000,000 natives, untold numbers of whom perished); the Congo (of 30,000,000 inhabitants at the time of its colonial take-over, 8,500,000 were still alive in 1911); India (open violence such the Amritsar Massacre: during the dispersal of an assemblage, 379 were killed and 1,500 wounded, in an episode which had a lasting effect on Nehru's political development); the Indians in the United States (the great anthropologist Henry Lewis Morgan had the courage to denounce their vilification); Nanking (the massacre by the Japanese); the Hereros in Southwest Africa (40,000 men, women, and children were surrounded, driven to the desert, and left to die of hunger and thirst. Neither the German Parliament nor the traders or missionaries protested. Report of the German General Staff: the Hereros had ceased "to exist as an independent tribe." The General Staff today is the same institution with the same traditions. General Heusinger, former chief of the General Staff and presently chairman of the NATO Permanent Military Committee in Washington, used the expression "merciless hardness"); Armenians (1,500,000 were

"Looking at Potatoes from Below"

driven from the place they had cultivated for more than 2,000 years; many men, women, and children were massacred or left to perish in the desert); and so on and on.

These massacres have a number of features in common. They are not usually committed by the hotheaded anonymous groups or mobs which we like to accuse, but by cold-blooded ruling powers, for material advantages. They are characterized by a mixture of commercial and sadistic motives, by cruelty, by the vilification of victims regarded as subpeople and not really human, by the failure —or connivance—of what one might regard as restraining agencies and institutions. The history books tell us little about these events, although much can be learned from them. Viewed against this background, the Nazi holocaust appears as the historical intersection of past vilifications and unresolved violences.

What makes the Nazi administrative mass killings so outstanding is not their numbers, their efficiency, or their cruelty, but the fact that they occurred in an epoch when nobody thought it was humanly or socially possible. Therein lies their deepest lesson. If it was possible then, why not again? What has fundamentally changed? The curtain may have gone down—but only for the intermission. No social scientist or psychologist had predicted that near the mid-century some 8,000,000 nonparticipants in any war action would be deliberately killed. Is it not indicated for behavioral scientists to reexamine their perspective and to realize how closely violence is interwoven in the very fabric of our social life?

A strong economic lever promoted the mass violence. The material interestedness involved the state, the big corporations, and countless ordinary people who profited. Until February, 1945, the police and SS bureaucrat Himmler met frequently with his advisory circle of thirty to forty leading industrialists, bankers, and other members of the economic elite. A high-level order from the central office of the SS addressed to the commanders of all concentration camps said: "It is self-understood that the first thing to be considered is the hundred percent economic use of the inmates."

The commercialization of mass violence proceeded along five main lines:

1. Slave labor

The German Euthanasia Program

2. Disposal of victims' property and personal belongings
3. Commercial utilization of human bodies
4. Supplying gas chambers and crematory furnaces as well as chemicals, for killing and disposing of bodies
5. Using victims as test objects for commercial products

Slave Labor

Slave labor had a tremendous, still vastly underrated importance, both as a way of killing and as a method of making profits. It was a matter not only of lives but of ledgers as well. As a report to Himmler stated, the concentration camps had to be shaped from their "one-sided political form into an organization corresponding to the economic tasks." Protocols of conferences are extant in which Himmler and Goebbels agreed on the principle of "extermination by labor." The rationale of the procedure—and it *was* a rationale and not irrational sadism—was to give the inmates as little as possible to eat and to make them work until they died of exhaustion or (when they could not possibly work any more) to kill them. There was only a short step between exploitation and extermination. This treatment was to be applied on the largest scale to Jews, Russians, Poles, Czechs, gypsies, prisoners of war, German criminals and political prisoners. Lieutenant General Helmar Moser of the German Army, former military commander of the town of Lublin, expressed it to a court this way: "The doomed people in the camp were forced to perform extremely hard work beyond their strength and were urged on by brutal beatings." Or, as a Nazi official put it: "Those harnessed to the labor process work willingly on the basis of continuous fear of death." Among these slave laborers were many children under fifteen. They had to work under the same murderous conditions as the adults.

A common practice was to have weakened prisoners, "slow workers," exchanged for sturdier ones. The weak ones were disposed of. They were sent to a place with mass-killing equipment and were killed. This was part of the routine of the whole industrial procedure. A regular weekly report of I. G. Auschwitz (part of

"Looking at Potatoes from Below"

the dye trust I. G. Farben) for the period from February 8, 1943 on, states that the SS and the industry managers "agreed that all weak prisoners could be got rid of so that we have the guarantee of almost full working performance."

Slave labor was used in three main localities: in general concentration camps; in plants and factories organized and operated by private industrial firms near and in intimate collaboration with concentration camps; in plants away from the camps, like the I. G. Farben factory at Ludwigshafen. The revealing term "company camps" (*Firmenlager*) came into general usage.

Inmates had to work long hours—usually eleven hours—including Sundays and holidays. From 1933 to 1945 the expenses for the SS for one inmate averaged about ten cents a day. That included board, clothing, "supervision," housing. Inmates were rented out to private industry at the price of $1 a day or, for skilled workers, $1.50 a day. That made a huge profit for the SS, which, as is often overlooked, became a very big commercial undertaking itself and also piled up enormous profits for the private industrial corporations from the cheap labor.

Executives, engineers, and managers of the private industrial corporations knew, of course, of their labor supply, its source, the conditions of work, and the final fate of the exhausted laborers. Many of them inspected the scene. In Auschwitz they were shown the crematorium. Some complained of the "terrible smell" from the cremation furnaces. In camp Dora there was a special building with a large chimney which smoked almost constantly, where the bodies of the laborer-victims were cremated. Nobody who saw the inside of the camp could have missed this building and its purpose.

In one of the subcamps of the Buchenwald compound, which was operated directly by and for the big electrical company of Siemens, every six or eight weeks 500 inmates perished. But the camp's quota of 15,000 laborers was kept filled by replacements. According to the minutes of their meetings, the directors of the Siemens company over a period of several years discussed the progress of requisitioning this slave labor to replace the dead.

Even in private industrial plants employing slave labor, where there were no concentration-camp commanders and no SS, the

The German Euthanasia Program

firms assigned to themselves the right to work people to death and kill them with impunity. For example, the Leipzig concern Hasag maintained three plants in Poland. In all three there were barbed-wire-enclosed camps under the surveillance of the private civilian company guards. Inmates were tortured, bitten by dogs set on them, and even literally beaten to death. One of the plants had its own place of execution for laborers too starved or exhausted to work any more. Even pregnant women were executed there. The SS had nothing to do with this. It was private enterprise. Involved in this routine of mistreatment and murder, and tried in court after the war, were managers, masters, foremen, factory guards, and twenty-three directors of this private concern.

The revenue from slave labor was carefully computed. According to official documents, the average duration of a slave laborer's life was nine months. (In Auschwitz, according to testimony of SS physician Dr. Muench, it was six months.) Each item was carefully figured out: the daily income from renting out prisoners; from this was subtracted the cost of feeding them and the depreciation of their clothes; subtracted also were the costs of cremating them. Added to the gain was the rational utilization of the corpse: the gold from the teeth; the clothes in which they were arrested; their valuables and whatever money they may have had on them. Especially to be added were the proceeds from the commercial utilization of their bones and their ashes. Finally the total gain was calculated on an "average duration of life of nine months."

Some of the large industrial concerns had an insatiable demand for more and more cheap slave labor. The percentage of such labor in some industries was at times very great. For example, at one time fully one-half of the 200,000 workers employed by I. G. Farben were slave laborers. The branches of industry which employed this labor were very diverse: chemicals, rubber, armament, electrical equipment, china, granite and stone quarries, construction, mineral water, textiles, leather, building, and so on. Among the better-known names of firms employing this slave labor from concentration camps are Krupp, Siemens, AEG (General Electric Company), I. G. Farben, Volkswagen-Works, Messerschmitt, Junkers-Works, Heinkel, Argus-Works, Continental Rubber, Daimler-Benz, Shell (Floridsdorf, near Vienna), and Bavarian

"Looking at Potatoes from Below"
Motor Works. Some commercial undertakings involved in slave labor are now closely connected with American capital, so that this period merges into our own economic system.

Disposal of Property and Personal Belongings

A further source of considerable income was that from the disposal and utilization of the property of the victims who perished. Apart from the property confiscated, such as furniture, furnishings, and similar items from domiciles, this consisted of personal belongings such as clothes, jewelry, cameras, and so on. This added up to a vast amount of material, which in the aggregate represented huge sums of money. There were shoes of every description, for men, women, and children (in Maidanek 820,000 pairs of footwear, from babies' shoes to soldiers' boots, were found); underwear; thousands of spectacles; men's ties; women's belts; robes; watches; mountains of children's toys; nipples for babies' feeding bottles; scissors; suitcases; artificial limbs; and so on. All these articles were collected, carefully sorted, packed, stacked, and dispatched to central places. The commercial and financial phases were negotiated and handled by the civil servants in the Reichsbank and the Ministry of Economics.

Utilization of Human Bodies

How human bodies were turned to profitable account forms a unique chapter in the history of violence. And it is not old history but contemporary history. Even in ancient times, what we call primitive people made graves for the dead; they did not utilize or barter parts of the bodies. That was left to the civilized barbarism of *our* time.

In the First World War, British Intelligence spread a false story that the Germans were making soap from corpses. It was left to the Second World War to make this a reality.

In Gdansk (Danzig) during the Second World War, a brick building was erected for a factory for a new branch of industry. Here methods were worked out for the utilization of human fat

The German Euthanasia Program

to make soap and human skin to make boots, briefcases, and bags. In the basement of the building there were large square concrete baths covered with zinc sheeting. Ten bodies were placed in carbolic acid solutions in each bath. Experts have established that among those who were shot, hanged or clubbed before being so treated, some still showed signs of life. In one room of the factory were big boilers in which the human soap was made. This was successful, and specimens of the soap (in pails) are still extant. The production of human leather did not progress so far and led only to semifinished articles of tanned human skin.

This industry was designed and organized by scientists and doctors. Even courses for production of human soap were given to other doctors from different concentration camps. Of course, such an industry was feasible only on the basis of a policy of mass extermination. The existence of this undertaking for the use of human raw material for soap factories and tanneries was no secret. Prominent people visited the place, including the rector of Danzig University, the Minister of Health, the Minister of National Education.

Gold teeth and fillings were taken out of the mouths of those who died or were killed in the concentration camps. No corpse could be burned without a stamp on the chest: "Inspected for gold fillings." This added up to thousands of pounds of gold.

Women's hair, and men's as well, was cut off, collected, and stored in sacks or barrels. Then it was sold, to be used for the production of felt hats, mattresses, and other felt products. A private felt factory in Roth near Nuremberg did a flourishing business of this kind.

The ashes of those cremated were utilized as fertilizer. That made a lot of fertilizer and represented a great economic asset. It was used on fields and in gardens. There were also special mills for the grinding of human bones. A very efficient mass-production bone-milling plant existed, for example, in the camp Chelmo, near Posen. Both ground bones and ashes were placed in large tin cans and shipped all over Germany for fertilizing the fields. Even a special method for using small human bones and ashes as fertilizer was worked out. It consisted of "a layer of human bones, a layer of human ashes, a layer of manure."

"Looking at Potatoes from Below"

Supplying Machinery for Extermination

The supplying of crematories, gas furnaces, and chemicals for killing and disposing of bodies became a lucrative business for large private concerns. No businessman seems to have had the slightest scruples about it. And with the introduction of gas ovens and big crematory furnaces, mass murder became industrialized. This is something new in the history of both violence and economics. Perfectly legitimate and highly regarded concerns took part in it. For example, a big electrical company, Siemens, devised and manufactured gas-chamber installations in which the murders were carried out. The company had a monopoly on gas-chamber electrical equipment. It introduced new and ingenious devices. Among them was a ventilating system by which gas could be drawn out and fresh gas blown in quickly. This made it possible to kill as many as 10,000 persons within a twenty-four-hour period.

Chemicals and poison gas, like Zyklon B gas (which gives off cyanide when exposed to the air), were manufactured for the purpose of mass killing in the camps by the big chemical concern I. G. Farben (the subsidiary firm Degesch). With these products, wholesale numbers of prisoners, including the spent slave laborers who worked in their own plants, were exterminated. In other words, you earn money by obtaining cheap prison laborers, and then you make more money by selling the means to kill them when they get exhausted.

Mass killing presented new technical problems. What to do with the corpses for instance? At first that seemed an unsolvable question. But it was solved by using the most modern equipment for burning garbage and refuse in a large city and transforming the bodies into usable products. In the city of Berlin it had been found that high temperatures—up to 1,400 degrees Centigrade—were needed to accomplish this. Exactly the same method was introduced in the concentration-camp crematory furnaces. In Maidanek, for example, temperatures of 1,500 degrees Centigrade were used. The crematorium there, a huge stone building with a big factory chimney, was the world's largest.

71

The German Euthanasia Program

Use of Prisoners as Test Objects for Commercial Products

Another economic gain from mass violence was the use of human beings as test objects for experiments with marketable pharmaceutical products and with chemical war weapons such as poison gas. A letter from an official of the I. G. Farben chemical trust to the Auschwitz concentration-camp administration is typical of the matter-of-fact use of human guinea pigs: "We have received the 150 women we asked for. Although extremely exhausted, they met our requirements. The tests were successful. All the subjects died. We are soon starting negotiations for another lot." Children were used in the same way. For example, six girl inmates aged eight to fourteen were infected with hepatitis to try out a new remedy for this disease. The name Murder, Inc., would have been more appropriate for the firms which supplied the installations and chemicals for the specific purpose of mass killing of civilians and disposal of their bodies than for the gangster syndicate which was responsible for a mere thousand murders.

Some of the cruel medical experiments on inmates to test new drugs did not originate in the heads of individual doctors, but were asked for and initiated by pharmaceutical firms. This combination of business, pharmacology, and violence is a significant sociological fact. There is, for example, the scene of the group of prisoners in the Sachsenhausen concentration camp marching—singing and whistling—under the influence of a new energy pill that was being tested for a pharmaceutical firm. They were marching like this to their death in the gas chamber.

These inhuman experiments are not a thing of the past. They are still taken for granted and commercially cited. One of the cruelest and most painful medical experiments in the Dachau camp was the immersion of inmates in ice-cold water. Some were given a drug; those in a control group were not. It was claimed that those who got the drug survived, while those who did not died. Now, two decades later, advertising specifically refers to these "cold water experiments" in promoting this same drug (which is, incidentally, of very doubtful value).

"Looking at Potatoes from Below"

The cheap labor furnished by concentration-camp inmates was an enormous economic asset. We cannot do justice to these cruel facts psychoanalytically alone. Slave labor did not satisfy any deep aggressive instincts; it satisfied the stockholders. The historian J. Schmelzer, of the Martin Luther University in Halle-Wittenberg, made an interesting sociological study of the responsible officials of the I. G. Farben concern who were involved in the slave-labor period and what positions they hold today. The study shows how the action phase of this mass violence merges imperceptibly into the respectability of the postviolence phase. An interesting sidelight is the fact that Friedrich Vialon, a high Nazi official who had to do with the renting out of slave laborers to private industry, is today State Secretary in the ministry for aid to underdeveloped countries.

What happened to the firms who used slave labor? Many of them, or their successors, are doing fine. Their shares are sound financially, even if not morally. Some of the prominent men and concerns involved in these sources of labor today hold more concentrated economic power than ever. This means that in the postviolence phase, violence was not resolved but was rewarded.

The Krupp concern built places of production near such death camps as Auschwitz. In the places of production, thousands of inmates were worked half—or rather three-quarters—to death, then in the camps they were pushed the rest of the way. The number of Krupp forced laborers in the original factories and the camp plants comprised at least 75,000 civilians and 25,000 prisoners of war. Alfred Krupp, head of the firm, was sentenced to twelve years in jail for the use and abuse of slave labor. Long before his sentence was due to expire, after four years in a pleasant prison, he went free. His release was celebrated in the biggest hotel in town with a champagne breakfast. He gave a press conference for more than fifty press representatives at a flower-decorated table and was greeted like a national hero. Asked whether he would repent what he had done, he replied that he had not thought out philosophically the ramifications of his conduct. Judging by what has happened since, we have not either. Today, with an assist from the financial and political establishment of the United States, he is head of one of the largest individually owned industrial concerns

The German Euthanasia Program

in the world. In 1957 there was a great celebration of his fiftieth birthday. As of 1965 the Krupp group had net assets of more than a billion dollars and was entirely owned by Alfred Krupp. The company now produces twice as much steel as it did before World War II.

This is a twentieth-century success story—success for the perpetration of violence. For since the violence of slave labor worked so well, financially speaking, it is an endorsement and a direct incentive for the future. In a wider perspective the firms which profit from the apartheid conditions in South Africa play a role comparable to that of the industries in Germany which profited from slave labor directly. In a typical year (1962), American companies operating in South Africa made profits of $72,000,000. That is double the average revenue from American investments abroad (11.8 percent).

What was in the minds of those who participated in one way or another in the administrative mass murders? According to the federal bureau charged with the prosecution of Nazi crimes, 80,000 persons participated in the exterminations. Of course, some of them were abnormal, sadistic, hostility-ridden personalities who acted from uncontrolled primitive drives. But in view of the very large numbers of participants in these massacres, the problem of individual character recedes into the background. Only social psychology can help us to understand this collective behavior. Many of these persons not only were inhuman officials but were officially inhuman. At the one pole were those who carried out the deeds; at the other, those who may be called the desk murderers, the intellectual originators. In between were the middlemen of murder. In vain do we look for any number of colorful, eccentric personalities. Instead we find a large gray mass of functionaries, bureaucrats, and rank-and-file killers. Here were the policy makers, the diplomats who made the orders palatable for foreign consumption, men who gave the orders, the transmitters of the orders, the organizers and supervisors, the civil servants, the technical personnel, the legal experts, the physicians (present in every concentration camp and acting like anything but physicians), the clerks, the workers, the approving bystanders and spectators.

It has frequently been stated that the population as a whole

"Looking at Potatoes from Below"

just accepted the political directives and responded passively. Sociological analysis of the evidence from the first years of the regime, when the mass violence started, indicates that this is not true. The people did not take the avalanche of authoritarian violence without question. We can reconstruct a whole fever curve: puzzlement, indecisiveness, refusal, illusion, awakening, awareness of the closing in of the propaganda and the violence, insecurity, passive resistance, disappointment with the wrong prognostications of the liberal leaders, emptiness, anxiety, hope of help from other countries, helplessness, resignation, toleration, disappointment, indifference, submission, fascination with the new dynamic regime, adherence. During this period while the victims lost their freedom, many intellectuals lost their convictions.

The central fact that stands out from the study of the administrative mass murders is the power of incitement. It can corrode the thinking of the innocent. People, practically all people, can be incited to violence. They may not all carry it out themselves; they may only help from a distance and tolerate and thereby foster it. But it is a fallacy to assume that the majority of right-thinking people are immune to these mass influences and that only predisposed personalities succumb to them. Even the good man, as George Gissing wrote long ago, "becomes ready for any evil to which contagion prompts him." If we place all our emphasis on the unconscious, we neglect the role of conscious manipulation.

Effective incitement to violence does not proceed as simple, direct suggestion or exhortation. It always has to be combined, as Georges Sorel, a political theoretician of violence, has pointed out, with a "myth." One such suitable myth consists in the complete vilification of opponents. They are the ones toward whom heroic hardness is to be shown. Along with the myth that the life of other people has no value goes a tremendous, pleasant feeling of superiority. An SS man put it this way in his diary: "How superior we feel after each one of the Fuehrer's speeches!" If the potential opponents are regarded as subhuman, as subpeople, their complete destruction becomes morally permissible and even necessary. We underestimate the absolute cruelty that can be engendered in this way and only in this way.

The next step follows with a certain inevitability. For both the

The German Euthanasia Program

higher ranks—the planners—and the lower ranks—the doers—it became a habit to use violence for settling tasks and solving problems. This habit became more and more ingrained. When Abe Reles, one of the executioners of Murder, Inc., was asked by the District Attorney, "Did your conscience ever bother you?" he answered, "How did you feel when you tried your first law case?" The District Attorney replied that he was nervous but that later he got used to it. And Reles responded, "It's the same with murder. I got used to it."

CHAPTER V
MEDICAL OATHS

The most famous medical pledge has been the Hippocratic Oath. It was a lifelong, unchangeable promise of the greatest profundity. It is important to understand the meaning down through history of "taking an oath". A person can make a promise. A person can make a pledge. A person can enter into a verbal, a written, a legal contract. All of these, in graduating order, add to the binding power of the promise being made. Another example was a phrase common years ago that "a man is as good as his word". In varying degrees, then, these pledge the promise-giver to a certain code of conduct, a certain duty.

Standing out, away and beyond all of these, was an oath. This in effect was written in blood. All of the above, in varying degrees, could be reversed, could be ignored, could be altered – as when a marriage contract, for instance, is dissolved by divorce. But an oath was forever. An oath placed that person's total life substance, honor and future before the world. There was no changing or backing out of an oath. Clearly, in modern times we have lost some of this meaning of an oath, and this certainly has been true of the Hippocratic Oath.

Hippocrates was a pagan physician. He lived 400 years before the time of Christ. His oath was destined to change the entire practice of medicine. Prior to his time, physicians, such as they were, performed two functions for their patients. One of them was to cure, but the other was to kill. "Doctor" was one name. Medicine man, shaman, witch doctor, and other names were also used. But it was to this person to whom you came to cure your ills. Varying degrees of magic, of potions, of prayers would be used. And the "doctor" would accept your payment of, perhaps, one chicken for services rendered.

That same "doctor", however, had a second function, and that was to do you in. That "doctor" could use similar magic and other methods to cast an evil spell on you, to harm you, or even to kill you. Since the patient, who had paid one chicken for the services rendered to cure him, was never quite sure that his enemy had not been there the day before and paid two chickens to the same "doctor" to do him harm, there was something less than full confidence in his doctor by that patient

The great contribution of Hippocrates was that he separated the killing and the curing functions of the doctor. In effect, he said, "Henceforth, a doctor will only cure." This comes down to us in the famous Latin phrase, *Primum non nocere*, "First, do no harm." The oath of this pagan physician passed unchanged into the Christian era and served as the ethical guideline for physicians until the last few decades.

Original Hippocratic Oath

The exact wording of the original oath is as follows:

I swear by Apollo, the Physician, and Aesculapius and Health and All-Heal and All the Gods and Goddesses that, according to my ability and judgement, I will keep this Oath and Stipulation:

To reckon him who taught me this art equally dear to me as my parents, to share my substance with him and relieve his necessities if required: to regard his offspring as on the same footing with my own brothers, and to teach them this art if they should wish to learn it without fee or stipulation, and that by precept lecture and every other mode of instruction. I will impart knowledge of the art to my own sons and to those of my teachers, and to disciples bound by a stipulation and oath, according to the law of medicine, but to none others.

I will follow that method of treatment which, according to my ability and judgement, I consider for the benefit of my patients, and abstain from whatever is deleterious and mischievous. I will give no deadly medicine to anyone if asked, nor suggest any such counsel; furthermore, I will not give to a woman a pessary to produce abortion.

With purity and with holiness I will pass my life and practice my art. I will not cut a person who is suffering with a stone, but will leave this to be done by practitioners of this work. Into whatever houses I enter I will go into them for the benefit of the sick and will abstain from every voluntary act of mischief and corruption, and further from the seduction of females or males, bond or free.

Whatever in connection with my professional practice, or not in connection with it, I may see or hear in the lives of men which ought not to be spoken abroad, I will not divulge, as reckoning that all such should be kept secret.

While I continue to keep this oath unviolated, may it be granted to me to enjoy life and the practice of the art, respected by all men at all times but should I trespass and violate this oath, may the reverse by my lot.

Oath of the Arabian Physician

This ancient oath dates from the 8th Century and played an important part in establishing the medical profession in those years. Its wording was:

I swear in the name of God, the Master of life and death, the Giver of health and Creator of healing and of every treatment, I swear in the name of Aesculapius, and of all the holy ones of God, male and female, and I call them to witness that I will fulfill this oath and these conditions. I will regard my teacher in this art as my father, I will share with him my means of livelihood and I will make him my partner in my wealth, and I will give him my wealth whenever he may be in need of it.

As for his descendants, I regard them as my brothers and I will teach them this art without any remuneration or condition should they desire to learn it. I associate together and regard as equal in the injunctions and in the sciences and in all else contained in the art, my own children, the children of my teacher and the disciples on whom the covenant has been imposed and who have sworn to observe the medical code of honor. And I will not do so for any other than these.

In all my treatments I will strive, so far as lies in my power, for the benefit of my patients. And I will restrain myself from things which are injurious to them, or are likely, in my opinion, to do them harm. And I will not give them any poisonous drug, if they ask for it, nor will I advise them thus, nor aid in a miscarriage. And in my treatment and in the practice of my art I will keep myself pure and holy.

To him who fulfills this oath and does not violate any part of it, will be granted the ability to carry out his art under the most excellent and favorable conditions. And he will be praised by all men in the future forever, while the contrary will be the portion of him who transgresses it.

The Oath of Maimonides

This dates from the 12th Century A.D. and emphasizes the need for Divine Guidance in the practice of medicine. Maimonides was a Jew, but his oath was completely accepted by Medieval Christians. He was a famous physician, theologian, philosopher and a confidante to the great Saladin, Sultan of Egypt. His oath stated:

Thy Eternal Providence has appointed me to watch over the life and health of Thy creatures. May the love for my art actuate me at all times; may neither avarice, nor miserliness, nor the thirst for glory, nor for a great reputation engage my mind; for the enemies of truth and philanthropy could easily deceive me and make me forgetful of my lofty aim of doing good to Thy children. May I never see in the patient anything but a fellow creature in pain.

Grant me strength, time and opportunity always to correct what I have acquired, always to extend its domain: for knowledge is immense and the spirit of man can extend infinitely to enrich itself daily with new requirements. Today he can discover his errors of yesterday, and tomorrow he may obtain a new light on what he thinks himself sure of today. Oh God, Thou hast appointed me to watch over the life and death of Thy creatures: here I am ready for my vocation.

Declaration of Geneva

After World War II, the Holocaust, and the degradation of medical science by Nazi doctors, the World Medical Association issued the Declaration of Geneva. This was an attempt by them, standing in the ashes of World War II and its atrocities, to formulate a modern oath. Its wording was:

I solemnly pledge myself to consecrate my life to the service of humanity. I will give to my teachers the respect and gratitude which is their due. I will practice my profession with conscience and dignity. The health of my patient will be my first consideration. I will respect the secrets which are confided in me. I will maintain by all means in my power

*the honor and noble traditions of the medical profession.
My colleagues will be my brothers. I will not permit
considerations of religion, nationality, race, party politics or
social standing to intervene between my duty and my patient.
I will maintain the utmost respect for human life, from the
time of conception. Even under threat, I will not use my
medical knowledge contrary to the laws of humanity. I make
these promises solemnly, freely and upon my honor.*

There is an obvious commonality among all of these oaths. They have
usually been sworn as oaths at the graduation and licensing of a physician.
It was universal practice throughout the Western world and, increasingly
internationally, that this or the Oath of Hippocrates was solemnly sworn
by medical students upon the conferral of their degree of Doctor of
Medicine. Then the decay began.

The virus of abortion began to permeate some in the medical
profession. This was noticeable early on, particularly among some of the
teachers of doctors. If a doctor was going to perform abortions, he or she
could not comfortably repeat the entire oath of Hippocrates, and so
quietly, progressively, medical schools began to drop the following lines:

*"I will give no deadly medicine to anyone, if asked, nor
suggest such counsel, and in like manner I will not give a
woman a pessary to produce abortion."*

An interesting example of this was in a seminal publication about the
Holocaust by Robert Lipton entitled *The Nazi Doctors.* Published in 1986,
this was a detailed account of the actual Nazi doctors in interviews with
those still surviving and the part they had played in the Holocaust. Lipton
makes a very strong point at the beginning that these doctors violated the
solemnity of the Hippocratic Oath that they had taken. The oath is
prominently printed at the beginning of the book, but guess what? Lipton
deleted the above phrase.

Back to training doctors. The next move after removing abortion from
the oath was to substitute something for it. Most commonly, when a
substitution was made, it was the equivalent of "I will do nothing illegal",
which coincidentally mirrored the position taken by the American
Medical Association after abortion was legalized in 1973 through the
Roe vs. Wade decision.

As the years passed, more and more schools simply dropped the oath
altogether. Not only was there an ethical conflict with abortion, but
increasingly with euthanasia. And so it has become increasingly clear that

the great contribution of Hippocrates, that of separating the curing and killing function of doctors is being abandoned. This ethic had lasted for over 2,000 years and had crossed the lines of all nations and all ethical and religious boundaries.

Now there are licensed physicians who deliver a baby in one room and kill an intrauterine baby of the same age in another room. Now there are physicians in Holland who go to great lengths to preserve the life of an ailing elder citizen on one day, and deliberately snuff out the life of another person the next day. What the ultimate end result of this ethical conflict will be, no one really knows.

Returning to the question of an oath, there has been a new and very positive development. Sparked by veteran pro-life physician, Dr. Joseph Stanton, a group of 35 distinguished physicians, attorneys, theologians and professors (including your author) worked together. In 1995 this group finalized an updating and a restatement of the Oath of Hippocrates. It is phrased in modern but dignified verse relevant to our times and is true to the original ethic. Its wording is:

Updated Hippocratic Oath

I swear in the presence of the Almighty and before my family, my teachers and my peers that according to my ability and judgment I will keep this Oath and Stipulation:

To reckon all who have taught me this art equally dear to me as my parents and in the same spirit and dedication to impart a knowledge of the art of medicine to others. I will continue with diligence to keep abreast of advances in medicine. I will treat without exception all who seek my ministrations, so long as the treatment of others is not compromised thereby, and I will seek the counsel of particularly skilled physicians where indicated for the benefit of my patient.

I will follow that method of treatment which according to my ability and judgment I consider for the benefit of my patient and abstain from whatever is harmful or mischievous. I will neither prescribe nor administer a lethal dose of medicine to any patient even if asked nor counsel any such thing nor perform act or omission with direct intent deliberately to end a human life. I will maintain the utmost respect for every human life from fertilization to natural death and reject abortion that deliberately takes a unique human life.

With purity, holiness, and beneficence I will pass my life and practice my art. Except for the prudent correction of an imminent danger, I will neither treat any patient nor carry out any research on any human being without the valid informed consent of the subject or the appropriate legal protector thereof, understanding that research must have as its purpose the furtherance of the health of that individual. Into whatever patient setting I enter, I will go for the benefit of the sick and will abstain from every voluntary act of mischief or corruption and further from the seduction of any patient.

Whatever in connection with my professional practice or not in connection with it I may see or hear in the lives of my patients which ought not be spoken abroad I will not divulge, reckoning that all such should be kept secret.

While I continue to keep this Oath unviolated may it be granted to me to enjoy life and the practice of the art and science of medicine with the blessing of the Almighty and respected by my peers and society, but should I trespass and violate this Oath, may the reverse be my lot.

And so time goes on. Whether organized medicine will someday return to its original ethical base, or whether all the modern forces conspiring to destroy its original ethics will succeed, remains to be seen. Clearly, the wording of the original Oath had lost some of its relevance, not in terms of its ethic but certainly in terms of calling upon Greek gods. We now have an updated wording which, hopefully, will find a solid place in future medical practice.

CHAPTER VI
THE DUTCH EXPERIENCE

If the citizens of a nation want to consider the possibility of legalizing euthanasia in whatever form, common sense should lead them to first investigate the Dutch experience. Here is a modern, educated, industrialized Western nation that has de-facto legal euthanasia in all of its forms. What has its experience been? How has this developed? What are the advantages and disadvantages that have become evident? What are the benefits, the abuses? What arguments convinced the Dutch people to legalize euthanasia? Have those predicted benefits been realized, or have those arguments been proven wrong? In essence, this small, tidy country has been a proving ground, so let's take a good look at it.

What Have We Heard?

Generally speaking, the treatment of euthanasia in Holland by the public media has been one of guarded approval and of a certain sympathy for the issue. We grant that most articles and commentators have shown a certain hesitancy to jump into an area such as euthanasia. Nevertheless, we are told in such reports that unrestricted euthanasia in the Netherlands is not legal and that it can be administered in only the most serious cases. Almost every account that your author has read or heard has detailed the fact that the Dutch have very tight regulations and restrictions. On their face, these are quite impressive and would lead one to believe that there would not be too many abuses.

Not So!

The actual facts are far removed from the story that we so consistently are being told. As a matter of fact, physician-assisted suicide has progressed to direct physician killing of patients. Euthanasia for the terminally ill has progressed to euthanasia for the chronically ill. Euthanasia for physical problems has progressed to euthanasia for psychiatric problems. Voluntary euthanasia has progressed to involuntary euthanasia.

The situation has progressed to the point where it has spawned the creation of several patient-protection groups. Many people today are afraid to be admitted to a Dutch hospital, particularly so, if they are of advanced age. Once admitted, the Dutch Patients Association will visit the patient. This group and others for a modest fee will watch over the patient so that euthanasia will not be administered without the patient's consent. One true story given to your author on his last visit to Holland will illustrate this problem.

A doctor in general practice admitted a cancer patient to the hospital and had completed the diagnostic studies by Friday of the week of admission. The cancer had spread and was probably beyond cure, but the patient was not uncomfortable and was quite able yet to live independently. She was told that they would be considering her case with consultants on Monday and then decide on proper treatment. The attending physician left for the weekend. On Monday morning he made hospital rounds, stopped to see this lady only to find another patient in her bed. He called the resident physician and asked where his patient had been moved, only to be told that she had been euthanized the day before. "But she was not terminal," he said. The answer came back, "Yes, I know, but she was incurable, and anyway we needed the bed."[1]

Historical Paradox

The current acceptance of widespread euthanasia is all the more surprising when one considers the events during World War II. The Germans had invaded Holland, and their occupation forces were everywhere. The Reich Commissar had notified Dutch physicians that they were to participate in the German Euthanasia Program. This was not the Jewish Holocaust, but rather it was the euthanasia program that preceded it. This program had been emptying out the mental hospitals, institutions for handicapped children and chronically and incurably ill people across Germany. Now they wanted to eliminate these "useless eaters" in Holland. The doctors' response was unprecedented.

. . . The Reich Commissar had notified Dutch physicians of his creation of an "Artsenkamer" (doctors' chamber) with obligatory membership for all practicing doctors. Most Dutch doctors feared that this was a way to force them to participate in the German Euthanasia Program. Of a total of some 6,000 Dutch doctors, 4,261 signed onto a letter that was handed to the Reich Commissar on 5 December 1941. In this letter they refused to join the "artsenkamer", as their consciences could not be reconciled with the Nazi doctrine. At the same time they took down the signs in front of their offices, making it difficult for the Germans to find a doctor. Some doctors were jailed and threatened with death, but the doctors faced this with a united front. They would not kill handicapped citizens. The Dutch doctors were the only group in occupied Europe that successfully resisted the German plans. Faced with this united front, the Reich Commissar backed down and withdrew his euthanasia request. Holland, through the balance of the war, did not kill her handicapped citizens and was, to this author's information, the only occupied country that did not.[2]

With this remarkable and heroic history behind them, one wonders how they could have done such a total about-face and only 40 years later begin to do voluntarily what they had risked their lives to avoid back then.

Holland has universal, cradle-to-the-grave medical care. It is adequately staffed with medical personnel and institutions. It has no extensive pockets of poverty nor large numbers of immigrant minorities. Its people are educated and cultured. But to this observer, one thing seems evident, and that is that most of the nation, with the exception of a tiny minority, has completely lost its religious faith. The two dominant religions have always been Calvinist (Reformed) and Catholic. Its flat countryside is dotted with churches so that, standing almost anywhere, you can see one or more church steeples. But most churches are empty. What had been a strong, commonly-held Christian value system that said, "Thou Shalt Not Kill', has to a very large extent melted away. Perhaps this is one of the reasons euthanasia has taken hold in Holland.

Back in 1941, nearly all Dutch doctors resigned from the "Dutch Medical Association" which then ceased to exist. The reason was that its board had accepted the ideas of the Nazis, and Dutch doctors would not kill. The current head of the Dutch Physicians League, Dr. K. J. P. Haasnoot, said that if any doctor had proposed such a thing (euthanasia) back then, he "would have been kicked out of the doctors' community"[3] and that neither abortion nor euthanasia had ever been an issue for doctors to even discuss. But in 1984, the new Royal Dutch Medical Association gave out directives to its members on how to practice euthanasia and still be protected against prosecution in a court of law. In 1996, the medical association confirmed this in an official brochure which repeated the directives. In essence it stated that a doctor can kill a patient if the patient requests it.

It all began when a doctor admitted to killing a patient and was brought before a court of law. The judge exonerated him and then laid down the first of the guidelines under which a doctor would not be prosecuted for euthanasia. Over the next decade, additional cases were brought – the doctors again exonerated, and the judge-made law became more and more codified. The result has been that there still is no formal decriminalization of assisted suicide or euthanasia. Rather, through these judicial guidelines, and others issued by the Royal Dutch Medical Association, and in new auxiliary laws, the Dutch have created criteria which, if observed by physicians, will exempt them from any punishment for being part of euthanasia of a patient.

Officially, at least, these criteria reflect an almost absolute confidence in the ability of physicians to make the critical assessments and distinctions necessary when considering the eligibility of patients for euthanasia.

Official Guidelines

According to guidelines issued by the Dutch Minister for Health, physicians will not be subject to prosecution if they observe the following conditions.[4]

- The request for euthanasia must come only from the patient and must be entirely free and voluntary.
- The patient's request must be well considered, must be repeated and persistent and must be maintained.
- The patient must be experiencing intolerable pain with no prospect of improvement. Such suffering does not have to be physical, but can be emotional.
- It must be performed by a physician.
- The physician must consult with other independent physician(s) who have experience in this field.
- It must be *force majeure*. This is a Dutch word which means that everything has been tried, nothing has succeeded, all alternatives have been considered, and now, as a last resort, the doctor must resort to euthanasia.
- All cases of euthanasia must be reported as such on death certificates
- All cases of euthanasia must be reported to the proper authorities.

But In Actual Practice

Any and all of the above criteria have commonly been totally ignored. The overwhelming public relations tragedy of the Dutch experience has been that these guidelines have been routinely reported as being an integral and functioning part of the program. Sadly, it is unusual to read or to be told that the guidelines haven't worked, for in actual practice, one by one they have first been ignored and then abused. The situation continues to slowly deteriorate, while the general public, even in Holland, remains somewhat unaware of its present scope. Let's examine the reality of present day euthanasia in Holland.

The statistics cited here largely come from a major evaluation of this program by the Dutch government itself. In January of 1990, the newly formed Coalition Government of the Netherlands appointed a "Committee to Investigate the Medical Practice Concerning Euthanasia". It was chaired by the Attorney General of the Supreme Court, Professor J. Remmelink. He commissioned the Institute for Social Health Care of Erasmus University in Rotterdam to conduct a nationwide survey. Three separate studies were conducted. More than 400 physicians were interviewed over a six-month period. Statistics quoted below largely come from this report.[5]

It should be noted that a repeat study, supported by the Royal Dutch Medical Association, was done in 1995. These investigators published a report of their findings in the *New England Journal of Medicine* in 1996.[6] The conclusion of this second study was that the situation had stabilized and had not gotten worse. A direct response to this was then published in the *Journal of the American Medical Association* in June of '97 by three physicians, including Herbert Hendin, M.D., a world famous psychiatrist, authority on suicide and author of the book, *Seduced By Death*.[7] These men expertly dissected the *New England Journal* article and the conclusions of the Royal Dutch Medical Association and used their own findings to demonstrate that, in those five years, almost every index had worsened considerably. Accordingly, let us proceed to examine each of these protective criteria.[8]

- *"The request for euthanasia must come only from the patient and be entirely free and voluntary."*

The 1990 report above indicates that of 130,000 deaths annually in the Netherlands, 25,306 involve euthanasia. It states that included in this are 1,000 cases of "active, involuntary euthanasia", which are usually a single, lethal injection done without the patient's knowledge or consent. Included also are the annual total number of cases of "involuntary euthanasia" (as distinguished from active involuntary euthanasia) which totalled 14,691. Along with the 1,000 cases above, these 15,690 included 8,100 cases in which morphine was gradually given in increasingly excessive doses with the intent to terminate life. And of these 8,100 cases, 4,941 (or 61%) were done without the patient's consent. Also included in the total of 25,306 were 8,750 additional cases in which life-prolonging treatment was stopped or withheld with the intent to cause death, again without the patient's consent. The report adds that there were also other cases, not listed, involving euthanasia of newborns with disabilities and children with life-threatening diseases.

- *"The patient's request must be well considered, repeated and prolonged."*

This criteria is obviously an elaboration and an extension of the first one requiring voluntary requests. It was added to eliminate any hasty "voluntary" requests that may be made in the moment of fright or upset upon finding that said patient has a fatal illness. The statistics for involuntary euthanasia above apply equally to this criteria.

- *"The patient must be experiencing intolerable physical pain or emotional suffering with no prospect of improvement."*

Pain – If it wasn't for this four-letter word, there probably would be no effective pro-euthanasia movement in any country in the world. In Holland the specter of agonizing pain and its merciful "release" by euthanasia played a large part in what has happened. It is still a major factor in the minds of most people there.

The central fact is that pain can be controlled. It can be relieved in all but the tiniest fraction of cases. The essential key here is the doctor. If he does not know how to control pain and cannot, or will not, take the time to learn, then the doctor's simple "solution" is to kill the patient when he cannot kill the pain.

It seems evident that the availability of this easy "solution" has been a major factor contributing to the fact that Dutch management of chronic or severe pain has been described by some as almost primitive, compared e.g. to England with its 200 hospices for the terminally ill.

- *"Euthanasia must be performed by a physician."*

This particular guideline has been almost universally observed in Holland, although there have been cases of nurses killing patients. In these cases, the nurses have been sharply criticized for their unilateral initiative. It would have been acceptable had this been done under a doctor's orders. The punishment, however, has usually been only a slap on the hand.

- *"The physician must consult with an independent physician who has experience in this field."*

This has offered no barrier at all to euthanasia, as the doctor who wants to kill the patient knows exactly which "consultants" will agree that this needs to be done. In fact, there are cases on record where such agreement has been given over the telephone. The government survey above revealed that consultation actually takes place in less than half of the cases where euthanasia is practiced without the explicit request of the patient. Further, one-third of physicians do not consider the requirement of consultation to be important.

- *"Force majeure"*

This phrase is unique to Holland. Experienced as your author has been in this field, across the United States and internationally, when first visiting Holland, this phrase had to be explained. It is a grab bag, a fall-back to justify any decision by the doctor. The doctor who is incompetent to treat his patient's illness then declares it to be a case of force majeure. If a particular doctor cannot control pain, then he calls it force majeure. Pick your own reason.

- *"Euthanasia must be reported on the death certificate."*

- *"All cases must be reported to the proper authorities."*

These requirements are ignored in the vast majority of cases. The survey above revealed that 72% of deaths where euthanasia was performed in response to an explicit request by the patient were falsely reported as "natural deaths". In addition, virtually all cases where a medical decision to end life was taken **without** explicit request were all reported as natural deaths and not reported to authorities. The Remmelink Report stated that euthanasia doctors want to freely do what they wish without reporting. "The problem, therefore, is not simply a slippery slope on which legalization of euthanasia for one group of patients inevitably leads to legalization for others. Legalization for whatever group happens to be first on the slope and cannot be regulated. Only after guidelines have been stretched, ignored or circumvented for some time does pressure develop to legalize whatever is already practiced."

One other consequence of this non-reporting is that it allows those who favor euthanasia to pretend that the practice in the Netherlands is well controlled and not abused. Dr. Hank Jochemsen, a well known Dutch medical ethicist, has said, "The majority of cases in which doctors intentionally shorten patient lives, either by act or by omission, remain unnotified, unchecked and invisible to justice."[9]

Patient Autonomy

This argument looms large among those who would justify physician-assisted, voluntary suicide. As should be evident from our critical look at the Dutch situation, the legalization of euthanasia has certainly not added to patient autonomy. Only in a minority of cases is the patient even involved in the decision. What legalized euthanasia has done in Holland has been to vastly increase the power of the physician over the patient's life or death. This has turned out not to be a patient decision, in most cases, but rather the doctor's decision, often not even shared with the patient.

Who Suggests?

Who suggests euthanasia? Is it the patient, the family, the doctor? We are led to believe that it is always the patient, but that is not true. Or, if suggested by the patient, it is only too often a cry for help. If this is responded to with compassion, the patient's request usually dissolves completely.

If the family suggests euthanasia, particularly if the patient is a continuing burden to his or her loved ones, there is no question but that this places substantial ethical and emotional pressure on the patient to get out of the way and cease being a burden.

In Holland, the doctor may suggest. What are the psychological implications of this? They are often profound. It too often gives a clear message to the patient that his or her situation is hopeless, that the doctor can do no more, and that only pain, fright and suffering lie ahead. Further, in a not too thinly veiled way, it truly is the doctor suggesting euthanasia to the patient.

Duty to Die

The patient who receives a suggestion from doctor, family, or whoever, that they are better off dead may well take this to heart. The aging parent who sees her estate rapidly melting away may be only too well aware that she is using up her grandchildren's college funds. The daughter who must stay home from her job to care for Mom, the son who takes a second job to pay Mom's medical bills . . . these and many other situations give a signal to the ailing elder that he or she is truly a burden, too expensive and, by continuing to live, is depriving her loved ones of life's necessities. The message received is that she has a duty to die.

But if euthanasia is not even a consideration, all of this is accepted and worked with. The experience in Holland has been very clear, however. With euthanasia as an option, many elder citizens find themselves making a decision that it really is their duty to die, and so they accept or even ask for their own demise.

Who Requests?

Well, clearly, euthanasia is not always the request of the patient who is killed. One finding that has been interesting in Holland and in polls elsewhere has been to separate out those who have requested euthanasia. It is clearly evident that the family requests euthanasia half again more often than the patient. Further, different members of the same family, when asked, respond sometimes diametrically differently, one from another, when asked whether Mother should be euthanized. The bottom line here is that the patient doesn't ask to be killed as often as her family asks that she be killed.

Only Terminal Illness

At the beginning, the Dutch insisted that euthanasia was justified only in a terminal illness. This was abandoned by the Dutch on the grounds that cases of chronic illness could also involve a situation of "necessity" equal to that of a terminal illness. Examples might be a paralytic condition or a severe crippling arthritis.

Only Physical Illness

For many years euthanasia was limited to physical illness in Holland, but that barrier has been broken. A psychiatrist was taken to court for giving a lethal cocktail to a depressed teenager who consumed it at home and died. Another well-publicized case involved a widow who had no physical problems but was deeply depressed.[10] A certain Dr. Chabot considered her case. She had been divorced from an abusive husband, she had lost both of her sons – the second only two months earlier to cancer. He did not treat her depression, but after two months decided that her mental state could not improve and prescribed a lethal dose of medication. Consultants agreed on this course of action. The Dutch Supreme Court, ruling on this case in June of 1994, affirmed lower court rulings that mental suffering can be grounds for assisted suicide. Chabot was not punished.

Clinical Depression

Far and away, the main reason people commit suicide is clinical depression. Clinical depression, in recent years, has been shown rather clearly to be a biochemical aberration in the body. It is not purely a mental disease. Drugs are available and, if taken properly, are consistently successful in lifting depression. (See also Chapter VII on Assisted Suicide)

Alternatives

One significant and very tragic result of the legalization of euthanasia in Holland has been the almost total lack of progression in developing compassionate alternatives to euthanasia. Holland, at this writing, has three small hospices struggling to survive. Across the Channel in England, where euthanasia is not legal, there are over 200 busy, functional and successful hospices.

In the United States, the American Medical Association, publicly recognizing inadequacies of physicians in treating pain, has launched a major effort to educate its doctors and correct the situation. Treatment of pain in Holland is primitive by AMA standards, and little effort is being made to teach clinicians modern methods of pain control. Why should Dutch doctors go to this trouble? Why should money be diverted to hospice care, when there is such an expedited "solution" available? The logic is impelling and in fact has governed the system.

The Doctor Decides

It seems clear that practicing euthanasia with legal sanction has encouraged doctors to feel that they can make life or death decisions without consulting even competent patients. An illustration used before the U.S. Supreme Court was "that of a doctor terminating the life of a nun a few days before she would have died naturally, because she was in excruciating pain and her religious convictions did not permit her to request euthanasia."

International Right to Life Federation

Your author is president of the International Right to Life Federation and has traveled widely with his wife, lecturing in 65 countries in the area of respect for human life, abortion, euthanasia and human sexuality. Recognizing the mushrooming issue of euthanasia in the Western world, we felt it wise to sponsor a number of international seminars in Holland on euthanasia. These have added considerable personal contact between ourselves and practicing physicians in Holland. Perhaps a good way to end this analysis of Dutch euthanasia is to relate several true stories.

True Stories

One was contained in amicus briefs to the U.S. Supreme Court. A woman who no longer wanted to care for her chronically ill husband gave him a choice between euthanasia and admission to a nursing home. Fearful of being cared for by strangers in an unfamiliar environment, he chose euthanasia. The doctor, although aware of this coercion, performed it.[11]

A pro-life physician friend in Rotterdam had been caring for a somewhat chronically ill elderly gentleman.[12] He lived independently at home with his wife who cared for him. He was not in pain. He was ambulatory but did need some assistance in daily living. This doctor had made a house call to check on him on a Friday. Diagnosing a case of bronchitis, he prescribed medication. On Sunday the old man became worse, and his wife called the doctor who was on call. This new doctor came, examined him, gave him a shot, and he was dead an hour later. Upon returning Monday morning, my friend was phoned by the near-hysterical widow. He hurried to her home to be met at the door by a crying woman who sobbed, "Dr. G., why did he kill John? John didn't want to die."

One more story will suffice.[13] There was a relatively wealthy elderly gentleman in a Dutch village who owned quite an estate. He lived alone with his wife. He was not ill but did require some care. On a particular morning, the clergyman visited at 9:00am. The doctor came at 10:00, gave him a shot and killed him. The mortician arrived at 11:00 to remove the body. The estate was quickly settled. The properties were sold and divided among the widow and the children who all moved to the French Riviera. There was not a single person in that village who believed that he had requested euthanasia. Yet the only witnesses were the patient, who was dead, the widow who smilingly related that he had requested it, and the doctor who was paid to do the deed.

So much for voluntary euthanasia in Holland.

Conclusion

It should seem crystal clear that if a nation is to seriously and objectively consider the legalization of euthanasia in any of its forms, or to any degree, it should carefully study the Dutch situation first. If ever there was proof of a slippery slope, Holland has demonstrated exactly that.

CHAPTER VII
ASSISTED SUICIDE

Why and Why Not

Chapter I explained why we should not commonly use the phrase "assisted suicide" but rather call it what it truly is – euthanasia. Even so, the term is everywhere today, and so let us look at "assisted suicide". This distinguishes the cases where someone else assists with the killing from those who do it themselves without anyone's help.

Attempts have been made in various nations, including the states of California, Oregon and Washington, to legalize direct euthanasia. These attempts failed. The culture of death people then came back and tried an opening wedge which they call "physician-assisted suicide". The same thing happened in Australia. In this chapter, let us consider the arguments being advanced for "physician-assisted suicide" in question and answer form, and in no particular priority. Of necessity, there will be a certain amount of repetition and reinforcement, particularly with the discussion of the Dutch experience. However, this format will make it easier and more logical for the reader to confront this issue. Let us, therefore, consider the arguments for assisted suicide.

What is the difference between helping a patient die in assisted suicide and in removing treatment so that the patient will die?

In one of the two cases presented to the U.S. Supreme Court in 1997, the U.S. 2nd Circuit Court of Appeals handed down an opinion that there was no difference. In addition, in the second case the 9th Circuit Court of Appeals stated: "We see no ethical or constitutionally cognizable difference between a doctor's pulling the plug on a respirator and his prescribing drugs which will permit a terminally ill patient to end his own life." The U.S. Supreme Court listened to this argument, considered it at length and read the briefs submitted. It then ruled that there *was* a significant difference and struck down that argument.

Subsequent to this, on June 4, 1997 an article in the *Journal of the American Medical Association* asked, "Does it make clinical sense to equate terminally ill patients who require life-sustaining interventions with those who do not?"[1] The authors, Drs. L. A. Alpers and B. Lowe concluded, "The U.S. Circuit Courts' reasonings are deeply flawed." and concluded, "Equating physician-assisted suicide with foregoing life-sustaining treatment could result in confusion for clinicians and patients, and undermine the care of terminally ill patients. We urge that the traditional, clinical, ethical and legal distinctions be maintained."

It's happening anyway. Why not legalize it?

Some have claimed that there are large numbers of patients killed, but that they are done without being reported.

Perhaps the best answer to this is – NO! This is not true. Such claims simply cannot be substantiated. There is a gray zone sometimes present with a dying patient when an increased dose of medication may contribute toward hastening death. But intent here is everything. The *intent* to keep a patient comfortable is one thing and is certainly ethical. The *intent* to bring about death is quite another thing and is unethical.

It's being done anyway in secret. With legalization, it would be done openly and there would be adequate controls.

Not so. If a doctor actually helps to directly kill a patient today, and that fact is revealed and proven, that doctor has committed a felony and should go to prison. In the event this were legalized, such an action would no longer be a felony, but, at most, possibly only medical malpractice. What makes anyone think that a doctor who will disobey the law today and commit a felony will obey whatever restrictions are placed if this were legalized? If he disobeys the law today under threat of greater punishment, he will more easily disobey the law tomorrow under threat of far less punishment.

In any case, just because a law may be violated, that is no reason to decriminalize. One need only think of assault rape or bank robbery, both of which are illegal. These crimes are being committed anyway, therefore we should legalize them? Obviously, this reasoning is false. Rather, the answer is to try to do a better job of enforcing the restrictions.

But the patient should have autonomy, should be allowed to be in charge.

Sorry, it hasn't worked out that way at all in Holland. The ideal of autonomy has a certain attractiveness, but it has turned out to be illusory.

Experience has shown that, in actual practice, in cases of euthanasia and assisted suicide, it is not the patient who makes the ultimate decision. It is the doctor. The doctor makes the diagnosis. The doctor decides it is "needed". The doctor obtains consent. The doctor decides when treatment should be stopped. The doctor decides what medications are to be used or discontinued. The doctor decides when the patient is to die. In assisted suicide, the patient has signed over his autonomy to the doctor.

Usually there is depression. There is an entire list of concerns – fear, anxiety, worry about finances, about pain, and much more. These all influence the patient's decision, even if the patient is the actual decision-maker. Add to these, internal pressures on the patient as well as the external, sometimes not too subtle coercion, by friends, family and the physician and we see that vulnerable people are not very autonomous.

But this is a private right, my individual right to choose. It really doesn't impact on others.

Yes, it does. It impacts on those in your immediate circle, but it also impacts on society as a whole. Among those close to the patient are those who are left behind – family, loved ones. It impacts on other patients within the sphere of influence of those around this person. If this person is helped to die, that paves the way toward an easier decision to kill off other ill, weak, aged or unwanted people. Further, there is the need for cooperation by friends and family, by the medical care givers.

For society, as a whole, if this one person is helped to die, those involved become, to some extent, desensitized and may well contribute toward additional deaths. Clearly, if we become desensitized to killing as a society, we will be able to find ample political, social and economic reasons for shortening other lives. Those most vulnerable – retarded, handicapped, disabled, sick, aged, poor, AIDS patients, drug addicted, etc. – are easy to devalue. Your private "termination" of the first patient can be like a virus that slowly spreads.

I want a death with dignity.

Would she want a death with dignity, or would she really want to live with dignity until death? Truly we should not equate dignity with control of bowel function or the need to be able to independently care for our own bodily needs at all times. True human dignity is internal, not external. True human dignity is the person himself. Illness does not destroy it. If a patient is treated with dignity by family and friends, he or she retains all the respect and dignity that their personhood is due.

But I think Aunt May does realize that she's quite a burden to her loved ones. If she agrees, why not help her on her way and relieve the burden?

Several thoughts are relevant here. If in fact Aunt May is the unselfish, self-sacrificing type who might want to get out of the way so as not to burden her loved ones, she is very likely a person who has been helping others all of her life. She, of all people, probably now richly deserves to be cared for, just as she has been caring for others. In contrast, usually the really self-centered person doesn't ask to be "put away" to relieve others' burdens.

But let our thoughts sweep widely. The classic example of getting rid of those who are burdensome was the euthanasia program in Germany that preceded the Holocaust.

Do we help to get rid of those who burden us?

Don't forget, each of our own turns will come someday. The simple, direct ethic here is clear. Each individual should be valued because of who they are, not by their physical condition. Just ask people in disability organizations. Ask those of minority races – of the "wrong" religion. They'll tell you. The only way to be sure that *you* will be taken care of in your declining years is for you to take care of others now. The only way you can be sure that *your* life will be protected is to protect other lives now.

But I can trust my doctor to do the right thing.

Look back to the Dutch experience. As many as one out of five people who die there are euthanized, directly or indirectly. Of those who are euthanized, perhaps as many as half do not ask to be killed and do not know that they are being killed by their own doctor. To legalize assisted suicide puts a tremendous power – almost an absolute power – in the hands of a doctor. Very likely, most Dutch people at the beginning thought they could trust their doctor. I'm sure they can still trust most of their doctors, but it's also clear that they cannot trust a *lot* of their doctors. With managed care today, when your doctor is off-call, a strange doctor will see you. You'll never really know if your own personal doctor will be at your bedside when that decision-making time comes. It certainly seems clear from the Dutch experience that people would be very foolish to completely trust all doctors. Human nature seems to be the same most everywhere, certainly in most Western countries.

But we do want to trust our doctors, and in the overwhelming majority of cases in the Western world today, we can and we do. But what if the doctor is given the legal option of killing you? What will that do to your trust in physicians who now care for you? It seems quite clear that, with

100

that knowledge in the back of your mind, it would undermine your physician-patient relationship. It certainly has done so in Holland where hospitalized elders hire others to watch over them so their doctor doesn't kill them. Would you want that to happen here?

Would you be able to trust your own doctor?

The advent of managed care throws a harsh new light on the doctor-patient relationship. Can the doctor be trusted to be your agent whose sole duty here is to do what's best for you? Or is your doctor an agent of some managed care conglomerate. Is he more of a bureaucrat representing their financial interests? Are their financial interests heavily weighted in the direction of having you die quickly rather than stay alive expensively? When you no longer engage and pay the doctor directly, when a distant third party insurance bureaucracy does, these are questions that must be asked, and these are legitimate concerns.

But wouldn't assisted suicide at times truly be the most compassionate thing to do?

Whose compassion? Is it compassion for the patient or for the medical personnel to relieve them of your care? Is it compassion for the family of the ill person?

Compassion truly is to seek the cause and relieve a person's suffering. It is not true compassion to eliminate the person doing the suffering. Compassion, then, means that we feel *with*, we work *with*, we suffer *with*, and we sit *with* the sufferer. We don't just get rid of the person suffering.

True compassion means to help overcome the fear of pain and, of course, to relieve the pain itself. It means to help remedy and correct any feelings of abandonment and rejection that this patient may have.

At least you should allow it if the patient is suffering intolerable and uncontrollable pain.

Let's separate pain from suffering. Pain is organic, physical, pain*ful*. Suffering is emotional, loneliness, despair, worry, etc. Pain *can* be relieved, and if your doctor doesn't know how, get another doctor. If your doctor can't relieve the pain of a loved one, don't kill the patient – kill the pain.

In the Dutch experience, of those who have requested euthanasia or assistance in suicide, pain was the major reason in only 5% of the cases. With only rare exceptions, people who previously asked for assisted suicide completely changed their minds when their pain was controlled. We must remember that pain is not only physical, but that social and mental problems exacerbate physical pain and make it more difficult to control. Effective pain control requires a team effort at times. Not just a doctor with a bit of morphine, but nursing care, counseling, a clergyman, and a concerned family.

And how is pain controlled? Well, morphine, or a derivative of it, remains the most effective single pain-killer. But it works best in slow, continuous or repetitive doses, often controlled by the patient. This method is far better than the roller coaster effect so common with the episodic giving of shots that so many of us are familiar with. Oral administration in titrated doses can control pain in three out of four cases just as effectively as injectable medication. Sometimes radiation therapy will solve a problem. Injections to block a nerve or, at times, even severance of nerves is an answer. Self-medication can be done through continuous infusion by a clever little pump, or the patient can administer small amounts when he or she begins to feel the pain return. To prevent pain when it just begins to come back takes far less medication than to knock it out after it has reached a crescendo.

Another pain control method, now in fairly common use, is to use cutaneous patches. Various medications are now given that way, including heart medications, hormones and, in this case, pain medication.

But this would be quick and easy – not a lingering and painful death.

The Dutch experience has taught us a lesson. The public debate in the State of Oregon and the passage of its law has also taught us. Such laws allow a physician to prescribe lethal medication which the patient then takes of his or her own volition. But what has happened where this has been done? Only 70% or 80% of those victims died from the medicine. The remainder had to be killed by their spouse, family, friends or doctor by methods varying from suffocation to a *coup de grâs* by an additional lethal injection.

Suffering

We must also distinguish between controlling physical pain, as above, and the fact that there is also emotional and psychological suffering. Loneliness, abandonment, despair, fright and worry may be present, and these may be worsened above all and most importantly, by clinical depression. In a very real sense, controlling physical pain is the easy part. Controlling emotional distress and suffering is much more difficult. But neither is a reason to kill a patient.

What of addiction?

As medical students 50 years ago, we were warned against using too much morphine for fear of making the patient a drug addict. This has been thoroughly disproved. The drug enforcement agencies of many governments, however, have not been fully informed of this. Doctors still fear, and usually rightly so, that if they use too much in the way of strong opiates (morphine, etc.), they may be liable to be investigated and/or even charged with illegal use. This <u>must</u> be changed. We now know that there is no upper limit to the dosage of morphine. An adequate dose of morphine in severe cancer pain quite simply is the amount of morphine needed to relieve the pain.

Do people need more and higher doses as time goes on?

Yes, some do. This is called becoming tolerant of the pain medicine. That is something quite different from becoming addicted. Over a long, chronic, severe pain situation, any one patient may end up needing doses five, ten or more times greater than they began with. But if the pain is removed, say by surgery, then they are not addicted and can discontinue the pain medicine.

Dr. J. Anderson reported that only 0.04% of patients treated with morphine become addicted.[2] A common example of this might be any woman who has had a prolonged and painful labor. How many doses of Demerol did she need? And how high the dose? But when the baby is delivered and the pain is gone, does she have a craving for the Demerol? Of course not.

But some of these people are so depressed that if you don't help them die, they'll resort to some other violent measure.

The people you are speaking about are almost certainly suffering from clinical depression. Clinical depression is now known to be a biochemical illness. There are effective medications available for treating clinical depression. Such a person must see a qualified physician, must receive medication, and then, by all means, must continue to take it.

Of people who succeed in committing suicide by themselves, 19 out of 20 are suffering from a depression.[3] 47% of suicide victims were suffering from a clinical depression, or varieties of it, such as bi-polar disorder and dysrythymic disorders, and some were afflicted with schizophrenic panic. Alcoholism added an additional 25% to those victims. 15% were recognized to have psychiatric disorders, but without a specific diagnosis. 4% had organic brain syndrome. 2% were schizophrenic, and 1% were drug addicts. These added up to 94% of those who committed suicide.'

Another investigation reported in the *British Journal of Psychiatry* came to an almost identical conclusion.[4]

It is well known that many, if not most, suicide attempts are truly a "cry for help". Commonly, such is true with cases of inadequate self-poisoning, wrist-slashing, etc. The victim's cry for help should alert those around him or her that the victim needs and should have care. Just so, a request for assisted suicide is very commonly a cry for help. It says, "I want you near me, I need company, I need pain relief," etc. Truly compassionate care will almost always answer and correct the problem. True compassion would not be helping to kill the patient.

What about a person in a persistent vegetative state (PVS)? Is discontinuing support systems considered to be euthanasia?

First it must be noted that this diagnosis cannot be made in a hurry. Total brain death can be confirmed usually in a period of days, but PVS can only be made after weeks, often months of observation. And some "PVS" patients have awakened years later.

Broad generalizations can be made, but only too often each case must be judged individually. With total brain death, all brain controlled functions cease, including respiration. The heart, however, will continue to beat as long as it is fed by oxygenated blood.

Brain death is usually defined in law as the total and permanent cessation of all brain function, including that of the brain stem. There are exceptions to this which include freezing and barbiturate poisoning.

With brain death as above, life support systems are usually discontinued. When oxygenation through the lungs ceases, the heart runs out of oxygen and its automatic pumping action stops.

In PVC, certain brain functions remain and respiration continues. The question then arises as to which support systems can or should be continued. A division must therefore be made between comfort care and treatment.

Comfort care consists of TLC, Tender Loving Care. This includes bathing, clean sheets, a warm room, a smile, a bath, proper positioning, pillows, food, water and other personal care.

Therapeutic care entails the use of drugs, surgery, etc. directed toward curing a disease, repairing an injury, removing a tumor, etc. Such therapy can be divided into usual and customary, such as giving antibiotics, splinting a broken bone and removing an appendix; and extraordinary care, such as heart surgery, organ transplants, etc. The care giver has always been seen as negligent if comfort care is not given. Extraordinary treatment has never been mandatory and should be judged in the light of many factors.

Some have now moved food and water from "comfort care" into "treatment". If then a decision is made to withhold further "treatment", food and water can be removed. If the doctor removes therapy, the patient sometimes dies. If the doctor removes food and water, the patient always dies, and painfully. Removing food and water isn't "letting him die", it's "making him die".

A sobering example of this was Karen Ann Quinlan. We recall that she lay in coma for a decade before she died. Early on, her ventilator was discontinued, but she then breathed spontaneously. All observers considered her to be in a PVS.

However, after her death, an autopsy showed no damage to her cerebral cortex (to everyone's surprise) but substantial injury to her thalamus. Was she then in a true PVS, or is there a possibility that she was in a "locked in" state and unable to communicate to the outside world? We'll never know. Her parents continued to give her food and fluids, but many others would have stopped this and "made her die".

What can we learn from religious teaching?

In the realm of religious faith belief, and an Almighty Who judges us, start with the Book of Genesis and Moses who brought the Ten Commandments down from the mountain. One commandment was extremely clear – "Thou Shalt Not Kill." That law has come down through the ages, moving totally out of a religious context and becoming what we now call a civil right, a right absolutely essential for the maintenance of a stable society. But such as it is a religious law, it does answer this question. We individuals are not the authors of our own lives, nor do we have the right to end it.

What's this business about a slippery slope?

Dr. Edmund Pellegrino, professor at Georgetown University, has offered us a clear picture of the slippery slope, which he calls a stark reality.[5]

• *The Logical Slope:* If euthanasia and physician-assisted suicide are beneficent for competent patients, can we deny this "benefit" to the incompetent? If death becomes a medical option, why can't we use it to solve other problems? If these measures become legal for those who are competent, it will only take one or two cases before a court to obtain rulings which will "equalize" and make these legal for incompetents, by someone else's judgment, of course.

• *The Psychological Slope:* Once a rule is relaxed, familiarity breeds contempt. There is a desensitization to killing, as has been so starkly evidenced in Holland. It moves from clear and rigid guidelines to becoming simply a matter of preference. Rules and principles become abstract, and there are ways around all of them.

• *The Empirical Slope:* Look at the Dutch experience. There we saw successive steps in relaxation of the criteria laid down by the judges. It was extended to non-terminal patients, to minors, to Down's Syndrome babies, to patients with mental and emotional problems, to severe depression, to dementia, then to non-terminal AIDS patients, and finally to involuntary euthanasia. Advance directives, so-called living wills, come to be used as a hard and fast indication of full consent. Because of the impossibility of enforcement, the situation slopes off, deteriorates and spins out of control.

Remember for a moment the law passed in the State of Oregon, allowing assisted suicide by physicians through prescription of lethal drugs. This was considered inadequate by the Hemlock Society who insisted that more lethal, direct measures must also be allowed for those who didn't die from the drugs.

And the next steps?

Movements are now afoot to completely decriminalize euthanasia in Holland. This "right" can then be extended to non-terminal elderly people, the mildly depressed and those who simply find life meaningless. It will be extended to those whose future life will be of poor quality after certain diseases have been diagnosed. It tends to focus in the future only on the degree of suffering. This justifies euthanasia and bypasses the effort to find the cause of suffering. It moves from those who have requested it to those who have not requested it. It gives the doctor a way out, if he is frustrated and sees family anguish in "hopeless cases". It moves toward substituting a family's standard of quality of life and their desires for the patient's standard of whether life is worth living and what quality of life is acceptable.

Finally, and important in the long run, it diverts attention away from pain relief and palliative care by offering a short cut to the grave.

CHAPTER VIII
DOCTORS

The Australian Medical Association opposes euthanasia
The Canadian Medical Association opposes euthanasia
The American Medical Association opposes euthanasia
The British Medical Association opposes euthanasia.

In sharp contrast to the pro-abortion position of major medical societies in Western nations, we find these same medical societies strongly opposed to euthanasia.

During the debates in 1995-97 over the Northern Territory's temporary legalization of euthanasia, the Australian Medical Association was a major factor in convincing that nation's parliament to reverse the law. Canadian doctors watched with great interest the national debate in the United States leading up to its Supreme Court decision in June of '97. The considered position of the Canadian Medical Society was quite clear. It opposed any form of euthanasia. The British Medical Association also opposed (July 1997) by an overwhelming margin.

The House of Lords of the British Parliament entered this fray with a clear position in favor of the Dutch euthanasia program. Properly, however, a committee went to the Netherlands and exhaustively evaluated that program.[1] This resulted in a complete reversal of the initial holding by every member on that committee. Responding to these findings, the British House of Lords then came out with a strong statement opposed to the Dutch euthanasia program.[2]

Meanwhile there was a major struggle in the United States. After two federal appeals courts ruled in favor of doctor-assisted suicide, the issue came before the U.S. Supreme Court. The American Medical Association took a very strong stand. Not only did it state that it opposed euthanasia, and specifically doctor-assisted suicide, but it moved very aggressively.

It submitted two amicus curiae briefs to the U.S. Supreme Court.[3,4] Co-authored with them were a total of 51[5] other major health-related organizations. An examination of the arguments in these briefs is very revealing. Its position was rooted in its belief that such an act is "fundamentally incompatible with the physician's role as healer".[6a] It detailed the fact that the state had an interest in protecting the integrity and ethics of the medical profession. It detailed the distinction between a patient's right to self-determination in ending care versus the intentional killing of a patient. It placed strong emphasis on the effectiveness of palliative care. It listed in detail the slippery slope concerns and the relative futility of regulating any such activity. It warned of the risks to depressed and other vulnerable patients. In its editorial analyses of the court's decision, the *American Medical News* stated: "Taken altogether, the court's decision deflates much of the rhetoric of the pro-suicide movement which has consistently confused individual rights with the misapplication of a physician's skills. The court's unanimous ruling is a major victory that protects both patients and the patient-physician relationship."[5]

The U.S. Supreme Court ruled that denying the presence of a constitutional right to assisted suicide still left the door open for individual states to legislate, but the AMA predicted: "There is not much of a legal vacuum for the court's ruling to fill. Thirty-five states have specifically banned physician-assisted suicide already . . . and most other states are on record as generally opposing the practice. Oregon is the sole state to allow it, and that referendum is headed back to the voters following a court challenge [note date of statement - 7/21/97]. State lawmakers can ignore the Supreme Court's opinion, but there is a better chance that they will study it carefully and understand why the bans should remain in place."[6b]

Anyone, any nation, any group seriously considering legalizing euthanasia, or even "physician-assisted suicide", would be well advised to profit from two long years of consideration of these arguments by the medical profession, lawmakers, churches, et al, in the United States, which culminated in the '97 Supreme Court decision. They would certainly benefit from studying the text of the two decisions. They will find of immense value the amicus curiae brief of the AMA. Accordingly, we print a number of passages from it and from other briefs submitted in these cases to the U.S. Supreme Court.

American Medical Association Brief

"Support for physician-assisted suicide was highest among those health care professionals least knowledgeable about pain and symptom management, and due to emotional exhaustion, least capable of empathizing with the patient . . . Doctors who had the least contact with terminally ill patients were the most likely to support the legalization of assisted suicide."

"Transforming physician-assisted suicide into a medical procedure would create momentum in favor of its use that regulation could not reverse. Were physician-assisted suicide to become a legitimate medical option, then a decision not to select that option would make many patients feel responsible for their own suffering and for the burden they impose on others. Once a patient can choose physician-assisted suicide, it is but a short step to ask a patient why he or she has not done so. Indeed it seems likely the patient would feel pressure to revisit the question repeatedly, perhaps daily. Many patients thus will experience and be helped by their families or physicians to experience their right to choose physician-assisted death as a duty to do so."

The AMA briefs repeatedly stated that "abandoning the prohibition on physician-assisted suicide will undermine efforts to expand the provision of palliative care to all patients."

And in a reason unique to the medical profession, the AMA stated that states have a strong interest in avoiding the damage to the health care professions and their ability to serve patients that would flow from an abandonment of the prohibition against suicide. The right to practice medicine brings enormous responsibility. "Patients come to physicians and nurses at times of greatest need and vulnerability, depending on them to respond to their needs capably and faithfully. Many patients, finding themselves badly injured and in the care of a physician they do not know, but whose license permits him or her to assist in taking the lives of patients, may understandably wonder whether that physician will act only to preserve their life. The ban on suicide helps insure that patients will never lose the trust that must exist for the relationship between health care professionals and patients to flourish."

"There is no evidence that increasing numbers of patients are dying in severe pain. To the contrary, the potential for management of pain has recently improved, both through the development of better techniques and through enhanced care delivery through hospice and palliative care efforts. The pain of most terminally ill patients can be controlled throughout the dying process without heavy sedation or anesthesia. For a very few patients, sedation to a sleep-like state may be necessary in the last days of life to prevent the patient from experiencing severe pain . . . When pain medication is properly administered, for most patients the risk of respiratory depression that hastens death is minimal."

"Given the increasing ability to control pain, it is not surprising that the demand for physician-assisted suicide does not come principally from those seeking relief from physical pain . . . Intolerable physical symptoms are not the reason most patients request euthanasia."

"This is not to say that all patients have access to, and actually receive, adequate pain relief and good palliative care. They do not. The delivery of such care is grossly inadequate today, and efforts to make such care universally available have not yet succeeded. The obstacles to delivery of adequate pain management include a lack of professional training and knowledge, misconceptions about the risks of addiction and respiratory depression with pain medication, inadequate communication, concern over criminal or licensure actions against prescribing physicians (Sub-quote from New York State Task Force)[6]

"It would seem that minority patients, elderly, female and poor are more likely to be inadequately treated. Medication and techniques that have been widely publicized and are effective require only modest resources. There is compelling evidence of the need to ensure that all patients have access to quality palliative care, but not of the need for assisted suicide in order to control pain."

"Most patients who request suicide do so out of concerns that in the future their pain will be intolerable, they'll suffer loss of dignity, become dependent and be an excessive burden. Such emotional suffering is real, but if the anticipatory and existential nature of that suffering is recognized and addressed, it can often effectively be alleviated. Along with this, there should be reassurance to the patient of a continuing commitment to attentive comfort care, along with assisting the patient to confront the underlying and unspoken fear of death."

"A full approach to palliative care addresses spiritual and existential feelings as well as personal and social burdens . . . A team approach is useful . . . If done, 'the desire for death passes, and patients say they have found unexpected meaning in their lives that makes their final days worth living.'"

The AMA brief emphasized that clinical depression is the greatest single factor as a predictor of desire for death. It then gave detail about the successful outcome of treatment of depression. It reiterated that the desire for assisted suicide is not a unique expression of untreatable pain by the dying but a far broader context of reasons: "Among all who commit suicide, only 2% to 4% are terminally ill." Further, "Only a small percentage of terminally ill or severely ill patients attempt or commit suicide." And these "are usually suffering from a treatable mental illness, most commonly depression."

Its final comment was that even if such assisted suicide were thought to be appropriate, "no one can predict with any confidence that this, if authorized, could be reliably limited to these few patients."

American Suicide Foundation Brief[7]

"No sound scientific or clinical basis exists for distinguishing suicidal patients with terminal conditions from other suicidal patients. Treatable, reversible mental disorders, usually of a depressive nature, characterize both. Both groups are ambivalent about the desire to die. Both suffer from extreme anxiety and cognitive impairments. Both have excessive needs for control, most dramatically expressed by controlling the time and place of their death. In both groups depression interferes with their decision-making ability."

"Terminally ill patients, including those who've expressed a desire to die, can have their depression treated and then are usually able to spend their last days in meaningful and pleasurable interchange with family and friends."

National Hospice Organization Brief

Those who support assisted suicide . . . "fail to appreciate that the final stage of life presents opportunities for meaningful experiences that could be lost without the state's protection of life and the prevention of assisted suicide, even among the terminally ill. Moreover, many terminally ill patients seek assistance with suicide, not because they cannot be cured, but rather because they cannot bear the physical pain and depression that often accompany terminal illnesses. These factors can almost always be ameliorated. Hospice care provides a proven, effective alternative to assisted suicide that is ideally suited to ameliorate the factors underlying the desire for suicide among the terminally ill."

"Hospices understand the psychological dimension of suffering and are committed to treating the depression and fear that surround terminal illness. When patients suffering from terminal illness are given proper palliative and supportive care, the desire for assisted suicide generally disappears.

Further, "Hospices provide substantial benefits to the patients' families as well by including them in the unit of care and by providing them with the counseling support and anticipatory grief work that has proven so effective in softening the blow of a loved one's death."

American Geriatric Society Brief

"Contrary to apparent assumptions, fatal illness does not have to mean severe pain and suffering . . . Most people die quietly, most often in their sleep. Hospice and palliative care programs have demonstrated that no dying person must live with overwhelming pain or severe physical symptoms. Severe pain affects less than half of cancer patients and only one-quarter of all dying patients. Sophisticated palliative care relieves pain for almost all of these patients and without confusion or substantial sedation.

"How society arranges services to support care of those at the end of life has profound effects upon how that life can be lived. Life just before death can be especially precious and important. When supported and comfortable, dying persons ordinarily accomplish important tasks, such as saying farewells, disposing of property, completing life projects, and enjoying their remaining days.

"Many persons consider suicide while angry and suffering. Such people, feeling worthless, often test others to see whether these views are shared, and if they are, this encourages agreement and in fact functions to affirm the denigration of their value. To offer assisted suicide at this time does not merely offer an option but also affirms feelings of worthlessness and devaluation."

It noted that extraordinary treatment for dying patients has changed markedly in recent years. "Resuscitation is now attempted for only about 10% of seriously ill persons who die in hospitals." Further, "the impact on end-of-life care, by managed care, is likely to include more reluctance to provide expensive care than to encourage patients and families to seek prolonged survival."

Finally, it noted that there is a claim that assisted suicide is now widely acknowledged, but underground. This organization "is not familiar with situations in which this is true, and these seem unlikely . . . There is little reliable evidence of the rate and nature of actual physician-assisted suicide." Most such claims, they say, are mere presumptions.

International Anti-Euthanasia Task Force Brief

. . . Warned that the oncoming tide of managed care is a system defined by "cost-cutting imperatives". . . which "rewards reduced levels of care". This could exacerbate the problem if the less costly and less time-consuming "service" of assisted suicide were mandatorily available as a constitutional right. This could create a scenario in which an agonized, depressed patient would ask for death, since their relievable suffering went unalleviated because of restrictions in available care, which was due to limited funds in their particular managed care program. "Legalizing physician-assisted suicide in a health care system in which financial incentives would favor denying care and hastening death would not serve the noble cause of individual liberty, but rather make a mockery of freedom."

Brief From California and Twenty Other States

This spoke to the existing right for the patient to refuse treatment. "The principles of bodily integrity and self-determination are so basic that they seem to need no justification. Nothing empowers the State to require a free-living, competent adult to always comply with medical advice. Such a rule would convert medical advice into medical tyranny. One searches in vain to find a case in which free-living, competent adults are restrained against their will and forced to submit to treatment by physicians. The law is entirely in the other direction. Competent adults are under no legal obligation to submit to offered treatments. The laws of battery and informed consent are barriers against unwanted treatment."

Brief of Religious Groups - Catholic, Baptist, Evangelical, Lutheran and Muslim

This brief noted that "opposition to assisted suicide is strongest among the frail, elderly and terminally ill, precisely those most directly affected by the issue."

Brief by Christian Legal, Medical & Dental, Pharmacists, Nurses, and Physician Assistants Groups

Quoted St. Augustine's denunciation of euthanasia as "a detestable and damnable weakness" and that, thereafter, "theChristian view that suicide was in all cases a sin and a crime held sway for a thousand years." Noting that in the pre-Augustinian time, recognized church leaders, including Clement of Alexandria and many others, condemned suicide. It concluded with a comment that the lower court's attempt at Biblical interpretation to support assisted suicide "illustrates the danger of judicial interpretation of religious doctrine. It is hard to imagine a subject less amenable to the competence of the federal judiciary, or more deliberately to be avoided when possible."

Orthodox Jewish & Rabbinical Council of America

. . . Stated that "the traditional Jewish position goes so far as to say that one ought not take any action that might actively hasten the death of terminally ill persons."

Catholic Medical Association

. . . Stated, "The inviolability of the right to life of the innocent human being, from conception to death, is a sign and a requirement of the very inviolability of the person to whom the Creator has given the gift of life."

It also brought to the court the long-considered and important conclusion by the British House of Lords after a full investigation of the

Dutch situation: "We do not wish that protection be diminished, and we therefore recommend there should be no change in the law to permit euthanasia."

Brief of the Christian Legal Society

Spoke to the rights of individual conscience to not participate, if made legal. "Certain health care professionals have substantial reason to believe that they will be subject to significant pressure from supervisors, insurance companies and employers, including managed care association, nursing homes and hospitals, to participate in the administration of fatal drug doses to patients." Many "have religious convictions against enabling others to kill themselves, as well as against killing patients, whether or not the patient has consented. Contrary to popular belief, individual physicians on staff at a hospital, clinic, nursing home or managed care organization often do not have sufficient autonomy to make medical decisions that carry significant economic costs for their employers. Employers who are concerned about a profitable bottom line are unlikely to allow employee health professionals the requisite scope to obey their religious convictions when the employers will be burdened by the economic costs of the employees' inconvenient religious convictions." This applied also to nurses, to medical students and other health care professionals.

Brief of Oakland County Prosecuting Attorney

This one speaks of Jack Kevorkian and noted that his actions "clearly demonstrate that the fears of opponents of assisted suicide are valid. Over three-quarters of Jack Kevorkian's assisted suicides involved people who were clearly not terminally ill. Kevorkian assists others to commit suicide based solely on his own determination of whether their request for his assistance is rational. He does not require that they be terminally ill or in unremediable pain. He requires only that they suffer some real or imagined malady that has sufficiently interfered with their quality of life as to convince them that their life is not worth living. If they are able to make a request for his assistance in what appears to him to be a competent manner, then Kevorkian is all too ready to grant that request. He engages in a facade of performing a medical procedure with adequate safety checks, but in reality, if his subjects are willing to have him assist them to commit suicide, then they invariably receive his assistance, and they die, whatever their true physical and mental condition." "Only by refusing to recognize a new constitutional right to die can this court hope to prevent an incursion of more 'Dr. Deaths' who will offer the sick, infirm, depressed and aged only the siren song of a painless death."

Brief of National Legal Center for the Medically Dependent & Disabled

This brief elaborated on how the United States' *National Americans With Disabilities Act* (ADA) would impact if assisted suicide were legalized. It stated: "If assisted suicide were recognized as a right for competent persons able to commit suicide by themselves, then the ADA would require that direct lethal means must be permitted for persons who, due to disabilities, are unable to kill themselves. Otherwise, persons whose disabilities render self-killing impossible would be 'excluded from participation in, and denied the benefits of' assisted suicide, solely because of disability. In sum, the present ADA law would require that homicide be allowed for otherwise qualified persons who, because of their disability, are unable to kill themselves."

Brief of Senator Hatch, Congressmen Hyde & Canady

It concluded by stating: "To affirm legalization of assisted suicide would require an extraordinary transformation of constitutional principles. Since such a decision would have no basis in constitutional text, no basis in original understanding, no basis in the traditions of the nations, no basis in the protection of a discreet and insular minority, and no basis in precedent, affirmation would stand for the bald proposition that the Constitution authorizes a court to invalidate laws simply on the basis that the judges disagree with them."

CHAPTER IX
U.S. SUPREME COURT

In the United States two of the states passed laws to forbid physician-assisted suicide – New York and the state of Washington. These laws had been challenged in the courts. Climbing to the federal district courts of appeal, one level below Supreme, it was ruled in the 9th Circuit (California, et. al.)[1] and in the 2nd Circuit (New York, et. al.)[2] that, for different reasons, physician-assisted suicide was a basic Constitutional right. These decisions were appealed to the U.S. Supreme Court. Forty-five separate friend-of-the-court (amicus curiae) briefs were submitted. The cases were argued in January of 1997. By a 9-0 vote, in June 1997 the court struck down these two earlier appellate court decisions.

It ruled assisted suicide was not a federal Constitutional right. It did not forbid it in the states, which remained free to make their own decisions. However, "giving" it to the states was not a mere legal technicality. The Supreme Court presented the arguments offered in support of assisted suicide and refuted them, one by one, in very emphatic fashion and very effectively. While individual states still retain the legal right to pass laws to permit assisted suicide, or even direct euthanasia, they will be hard put to justify either in the face of these towering opinions. These rulings are all the more impressive when one recalls, in contrast, that the 1973 *Roe vs. Wade* decision legalizing abortion was by the same court.

For anyone really interested in this subject, the entire rulings are well worth reading. We print below a portion of the official syllabus of each of the two cases decided. These are historic decisions which should have a lasting influence on this issue throughout the world.

SUPREME COURT OF THE UNITED STATES
Syllabus
Washington v. Glucksberg

(a) An examination of our Nation's history, legal traditions, and practices demonstrates that Anglo-American common law has punished or otherwise disapproved of assisting suicide for over 700 years; that rendering such assistance is still a crime in almost every State; that such prohibitions have never contained exceptions for those who were near death; that the prohibitions have in recent years been reexamined and, for the most part, reaffirmed in a number of States; and that the President recently signed the Federal Assisted Suicide Funding Restriction Act of 1997, which prohibits the use of federal funds in support of physician-assisted suicide. Pp. 5-15.

(b) In light of that history, this Court's decisions lead to the conclusion that respondents' asserted "right" to assistance in committing suicide is not a fundamental liberty interest protected by the Due Process Clause. The Court's established method of substantive-due-process analysis has two primary features: First, the Court has regularly observed that the Clause specially protects those fundamental rights and liberties which are, objectively, deeply rooted in this Nation's history and tradition. E.g., *Moore v. East Cleveland*, 431 U.S. 494, 503 (plurality opinion). Second, the Court has required a "careful description" of the asserted fundamental liberty interest. E.G., *Reno v. Flores*, 507 U.S. 292, 302. The Ninth Circuit's and respondents' various descriptions of the interest here at stake, e.g., a right to "determin[e] the time and manner of one's death," the "right to die," a "liberty to choose how to die," a right to "control of one's final days," "the right to choose a humane, dignified death," and "the liberty to shape death" – run counter to that second requirement. Since the Washington statute prohibits "aid[ing] another person to attempt suicide," the question before the Court is more properly characterized as whether the "liberty" specially protected by the Clause includes a right to commit suicide which itself includes a right to assistance in doing so. This asserted right has no place in our Nation's traditions, given the country's consistent, almost universal, and continuing rejection of the right, even for terminally ill, mentally competent adults. To hold for respondents, the Court would have to reverse centuries of legal doctrine and practice, and strike down the considered policy choice of almost every State. Respondents' contention that the asserted interest *is* consistent with this Court's substantive-due-process cases, if not with this Nation's history and practice, is unpersuasive. The constitutionally protected right to refuse lifesaving hydration and nutrition that was discussed in *Cruzan, supra*, at 279, was not simply deduced from abstract concepts of personal autonomy, but was instead grounded in the Nation's history and traditions, given the common-law rule that forced medication was a battery, and the long legal tradition protecting the decision to refuse unwanted medical treatment. And although *Casey* recognized that many of the rights and liberties protected by the Due Process Clause sound in personal autonomy, 505 U.S., at 852, it does not follow that any and all important, intimate, and personal decisions are so protected, see *San Antonio School Dist. v. Rodriguez*, 411 U.S. 1, 33-34. *Casey* did not suggest otherwise. Pp. 15-24.

(c) The constitutional requirement that Washington's assisted-suicide ban be rationally related to legitimate government interests, see e.g., *Heller v. Doe*, 509 U.S. 312, 319-320, is unquestionably met here. These interests include prohibiting intentional killing and preserving human life; preventing the serious public-health problem of suicide, especially among the young, the elderly, and those suffering from untreated pain or from depression or other mental disorders; protecting the medical profession's integrity and ethics and maintaining physicians' role as their patients' healers; protecting the poor, the elderly, disabled persons, the terminally ill, and persons in other vulnerable groups from indifference, prejudice, and psychological and financial pressure to end their lives; and avoiding a possible slide towards voluntary and perhaps even involuntary euthanasia. The relative strengths of these various interests need not be weighed exactingly, since they are unquestionably important and legitimate, and the law at issue is at least reasonably related to their promotion and protection. Pp. 24-31.

SUPREME COURT OF THE UNITED STATES
Syllabus
Vacco v. Quill

(a) The Equal Protection Clause embodies a general rule that States must treat like cases alike but may treat unlike cases accordingly, e.g., *Plyler v. Doe*, 457 U.S. 202, 216. The New York statutes outlawing assisted suicide neither infringe fundamental rights nor involve suspect classifications, e.g., *Washington v. Glucksberg, ante,* ƒat 14-24, and are therefore entitled to a strong presumption of validity, *Heller v. Doe*, 509 U.S. 312, 319. On their faces, neither the assisted-suicide ban nor the law permitting patients to refuse medical treatment treats anyone differently from anyone else or draws any distinctions between persons. *Everyone*, regardless of physical condition, is entitled, if competent, to refuse unwanted lifesaving medical treatment; *no one* is permitted to assist a suicide. Generally, laws that apply evenhandedly to all unquestionably comply with equal protection, e.g., *New York City Transit Authority v. Beazer*, 440 U.S. 568, 587. This Court disagrees with the Second Circuit's submission that ending or refusing lifesaving medical treatment "is nothing more nor less than assisted suicide." The distinction between letting a patient die and making that patient die is important, logical, rational, and well established: It comports with fundamental legal principles of causation, see, e.g., *People v. Kevorkian*, 447 Mich. 436, 470-472, 527 N.W. 2d 714, 728, cert. denied, 514 U.S. 1083, and intent, see, e.g., *United States v. Bailey*, 444 U.S. 394, 403-406; has been recognized, at least implicitly, by this Court in *Cruzan v. Director, Mo. Dept. of Health*, 497 U.S. 261, 278-280; *id.*, at 287-288 (O'Connor, J., concurring); and has been widely recognized and endorsed in the medical profession, the state courts, and the overwhelming majority of state legislatures, which, like New York's, have permitted the former while prohibiting the latter. The Court therefore disagrees with respondents' claim that the distinction is "arbitrary" and "irrational". The line between the two acts may not always be clear, but certainty is not required, even were it possible. Logic and contemporary practice support New York's judgment that the two acts are different, and New York may therefore, consistent with the Constitution, treat them differently. Pp. 3-13.

(b) New York's reasons for recognizing and acting ton the distinction between refusing treatment and assisting a suicide – including prohibiting intentional killing and preserving life; preventing suicide; maintaining physicians' role as their patients' healers; protecting vulnerable people from indifference, prejudice and psychological and financial pressure to end their lives; and avoiding a possible slide towards euthanasia – are valid and important public interests that easily satisfy the constitutional requirement that a legislative classification bear a rational relation to some legitimate end. See *Glucksberg, ante.*, Pp. 13-14.

Comment

To say that this court decision was momentous is a gross understatement. It could have been the *Roe vs. Wade* of euthanasia, declaring that direct euthanasia was a basic constitutional right. This would have legalized it throughout the entire United States and very possibly been the springboard for legalization throughout the world. In fact it very effectively near totally condemned it. It did stop short of "finding" a new federal constitutional right to forbid it. It occasioned the most indepth and lengthy argument of this issue that had ever happened before in world history.

Forty-five different friend-of-the-court briefs against "assisted suicide" and euthanasia were filed in one or both of the cases before the court. One of them, the brief by the American Medical Association, had 51 organizations co-signing. It is probably accurate to say that every possible argument posed for euthanasia, in recent times, was met and answered by this unprecedented number of amicus briefs. Another feature was that the briefs generally did not overlap. They did not cover similar ground. Rather, in a well coordinated effort by the National Legal Center for the Medically Dependent & Disabled in Indianapolis, Indiana, literally the entire legal resources of the pro-life movement, of the medical establishment, of the churches, and more, were marshalled to present every possible pro-life argument to the Supreme Court.

The briefs were from medical organizations and nurses, from allied groups such as the Suicide Foundation, Geriatric Hospital and hospice organizations. They were from members of the U.S. Congress, from the states themselves, from bio-ethicists, disability rights groups, many different religious organizations from different religions, from pro-life legal defense funds, pro-family, pro-life organizations and more.

An excellent summary using verbatim quotes from these friend-of-the-court, amicus briefs is available in the 1997 summer edition of *Issues in Law & Medicine*, Vol. 13, No. 1.

CHAPTER X
OREGON

The State of Oregon confirmed the legalization of physician-assisted suicide in November 1997 by a statewide referendum. Because of all of the currents preceding it, as detailed in the previous chapters, it is imperative that we take a closer look at the dynamics that led to this.

Bear in mind that this law had been passed by an earlier referendum in 1994 by a vote of only 51 to 49. Pro-life forces had challenged the law in the courts and prevented it from becoming operational until the eve of the repeat vote in November 1997. This vote reaffirmed the law by a vote of 60 to 40.

Even with this seemingly decisive vote, it is important to examine the dynamics of this vote for, in many ways, this was quite an atypical situation, not necessarily one that will be repeated elsewhere.

Scarcely a few days after the final vote was announced, a new and unexpected development occurred. A federal department, the U.S. Drug Enforcement Administration, issued a directive that in effect completely nullified the law.

Let's examine this more closely.

History

It is a recognized fact that the three West Coast states of California, Oregon and Washington contain the most liberal population in the United States and, in that sense, are quite atypical as compared to the rest of the nation. Therefore, it was logical that pro-euthanasia forces had concentrated their efforts on the West Coast, knowing that they had far less chance of success in any of the other states.

The first attempt was in California. A certain number of signatures had to be obtained to place this on the ballot for a state-wide initiative. That attempt failed because of lack of sufficient signatures. In 1992 an attempt was made again. Sufficient signatures were obtained, but the voters of

California rejected that attempt to legalize euthanasia.

The State of Washington also had an initiative referendum in 1991 which rejected euthanasia. Both the states of California and Washington had laws forbidding assisted suicide. Washington's ultimately found its way to the Supreme Court and is explained in detail in Chapter IX which upheld the validity of that law.

Other States

Thirty-seven of the fifty states have statutes that forbid assisted suicide. Most of the others forbid through common law or court precedent. In recent challenges to the laws of Michigan and Florida, such statutes were upheld by their State Supreme Courts. The case of Michigan is atypical in that, while there is a law forbidding assisted suicide, Mr. Kevorkian has been exonerated in the three attempts to punish him through a criminal proceeding.

The Oregon Law

Oregon's law now authorizes a physician to write a prescription for a lethal drug to be taken by the patient. Its laws forbid lethal injections by the physician. It has been generally accepted that the reason for failure to pass the earlier attempts to legalize euthanasia was that these proposals included lethal injections. This law, then, spoke only to "assisted" suicide, with the doctor writing the prescription and the patient taking the lethal medicine voluntarily. The law requires that the person involved must be terminally ill and have less than six months to live. If clinically depressed, the doctor must refer the patient to a psychiatrist, as the patient must be able to make a rational decision. There is a fifteen-day waiting period between the patient's request for the drug and the time the medicine can be obtained from a pharmacist. Pharmacists have proposed that the prescription specifically state that this is for assisted suicide, so the pharmacist knows, when filling the prescription, exactly what it is for and thus becomes complicit in the act.

Pro-Life Reaction

Pro-life reaction to the vote reflected great distress and disappointment. The nationwide pro-life, pro-family organization, Focus on the Family's Carrie Gordon, said that Oregon votes had "unleashed a force in this nation too powerful for man to control . . . There is no question that physician-assisted suicide activists will interpret this tragic vote as a clarion call to push their death agenda in 49 other states. Oregon has now stepped out as the only place in the world that has legalized physician-assisted suicide. The message from Oregon is clear – doctors now have a green light to kill their patients. To the infirm, depressed and terminally ill, beware. You can no longer trust the law to protect your right to live. This unprecedented vote puts countless citizens in Oregon and around the nation at risk for an untimely death . . . Oregon's approval of state-sanctioned killing perverts the practice of medicine and opens the door for coercion of vulnerable, suffering Americans to 'choose' an early death by profit-motivated health care companies, misguided physicians, and even well meaning family members. In this age of skyrocketing health care costs and desperate cost-containing attempts, an early death may become a reasonable substitute for treatment and care."

The American Medical Association's Chairman of the Board of Trustees, Dr. Thomas Reardon, called the vote "a serious blow to health and safety . . . Further, it sets a dangerous precedent for other states considering similar initiatives that physician-assisted suicide is an acceptable option for patients in the last phase of life . . . We all have rights at the end of life that preclude us from having to resort to physician-assisted suicide. Not only is it our duty to educate ourselves, our loved ones and the public regarding these existing rights, it is our obligation to ensure that these rights are honored."

Bernard Cardinal Law, Chairman of the U.S. Bishops Committee for Pro-Life Activities, called this a tragedy for all Americans, but "most of all, it is a tragedy for seriously ill patients who deserve better for their real needs, not an invitation to suicide" . . . He predicted "that if the law stands, the right to die will quickly become the duty to die." The Oregon Catholic Conference, one of the spearheads of the pro-life campaign, called this "a tragic day for Oregon, the nation and the world . . . Oregon has become the first jurisdiction in the world to fully embrace the culture of death . . . May God have mercy on us and on our nations."

The National Right to Life Committee's statement said, "Euthanasia in Oregon will not remain 'voluntary' for long. All it will take is for a court to rule that denying 'assisted suicide' to people who have never asked to die, but are unable to speak for themselves, violates state constitutional 'equal protection' provisions. This is exactly what courts have done in the past concerning denial of life-saving medical treatment."

Americans United for Life, a national pro-life public interest law firm, stated, "Oregon is now the most dangerous place in the country in which to fall terminally ill . . . The experience of the Netherlands demonstrates that what starts out as voluntary requests for assistance in dying, quickly and inexorably leads to involuntary termination of those who are deemed to be less than 'perfect' . . . A society that embraces physician-assisted suicide for the terminally ill is a society that also declares war on the elderly, the poor and the disabled who now are at great risk. Others will decide that their lives are not worth living and attempt to convince them that the 'dignified and responsible' thing to do is to seek their own death . . . 'Do your duty and die' could now become the outspoken but clear message to the vulnerable."

The Christian Medical & Dental Society echoed much of the above, emphasizing that the "right to die" will soon translate into the "duty to die" and put the elderly, handicapped, poor and others at particular risk. Noting, as did others, that "hospices, pain management and truly compassionate, loving care offer ethical alternatives to killing the patient. Effective use of these alternatives renders physician-assisted suicide unnecessary."

Other Reaction

After passage of the law, considerable professional comment ensued regarding a physician's ability to predict that the patient could only live six months. There was also widespread questioning about the ability of a physician to judge whether or not the patient was depressed, as the law says that doctors should order psychiatric counseling for a patient who appears to be so impaired. In addition, the law only applies to "Oregon residents" but does not set requirements for "residence".

All of this applies to those who might be judged to be average, conscientious, clinical physicians. With the Dutch experience behind us, it should be rather easy to predict that a certain number of physicians will find little problem with their consciences in making the above decisions for a patient regardless of the limiting conditions in the law, and regardless of the fact that the campaign showed that 70% of the doctors fail to and are unable to diagnose clinical depression.

Why Voters Approved

A central factor was the issue of <u>personal autonomy</u>. Oregon is the least churched state in the union, estimates being that fewer than one in four have a church affiliation. The entire politically correct concept of unlimited personal choice was a major factor in the decision-making of the majority.

<u>Anti-Catholic</u>, specifically, but anti-religious bias generically, was a major factor. The pro-suicide radio ads concentrated heavily on indicting "outside religious forces" coming into the state with bundles of money to impose Catholic doctrine on unwilling citizens. The labeling of those opposing the permissive statute was quite successful in eliminating, to a large extent, the credibility of "those people". Hard-hitting TV ads from the pro-life side should have had more impact than they did. These partly failed because the pro-euthanasia people neutralized their impact by

denigrating the sources that paid for the ads, i.e., "those religious people who want to impose their morality on all of us."

<u>Parochial pride</u>: Pro-euthanasia people successfully played on the theme that local Oregonian people were more advanced in their thinking than other states and that they could prove this by being the first ones to pass such a progressive law.

<u>Resentment at having to vote again</u>: This was a successful theme that will not apply to a vote in any other state. TV ads reminded them that the legislature was attempting to overturn a law passed already by the people. The attempt was held up as an attempt by the legislature and others to "take your rights away. They're making you vote again after you have already chosen by an earlier vote. This is an insult to voters", they were told.

<u>It doesn't always work</u>: Pro-lifers noted that an oral dose of lethal medication was often not lethal and that the patient lingered and had to be ultimately killed by a more direct method such as smothering. The pro-euthanasia answer was essentially "so what? Much the same thing happens now through disease."

At least some confusion was engendered by the <u>choice of a 'yes' or 'no'</u> on the ballot. If you voted 'no', it meant that you wanted to continue euthanasia. If you voted 'yes', it meant that you wanted to reverse the law and stop it. This probably cut both ways, however, and certainly did not account for the heavy majority margin.

Finally, pro-death forces largely convinced the voters that the law did contain adequate safeguards against "abuses".

In summary, it would seem that the major arguments that carried the day were the issues of personal autonomy, the fabricated, somewhat anger at having to vote again, and certainly anti-religious bias after having accepted the pro-euthanasia argument that this was only a question of religious belief.

<u>Possible broadening</u>? Adding to the news was worry over future legal challenges to the law that could broaden it. Existing legal precedents in many states hold that if a competent person has certain "rights", then Constitutional guarantees of equal protection require that a guardian must be permitted to make the same choice on behalf of children or incompetent adults. If a court does so decide, then involuntary euthanasia could become legal in Oregon.

<u>A silver lining</u>: There was some very positive fallout that should not be overlooked. Australia, through the heroic efforts of pro-life forces there, had experienced much the same. same. Just so, much good was also accomplished in Oregon.

"Without this lengthy and highly publicized campaign," the executive director of Oregon Right to Life, Gayle Atteberry, commented, "Oregon would have sleepily accepted the law, flaws and all, and assisted suicide would have easily worked its way into the fabric of our life. The voices speaking against it would have barely received notice. But because of the campaign, the deadly flaws of this law are known to all. Because of this knowledge, assisted suicide will be more hesitantly used, and in many cases not used at all. Because of the campaign, the Oregon Medical Association went from neutrality to being opposed. Because of the campaign, those in the medical community who are against assisted suicide have become solid and outspoken. Physicians "in the middle" have been given encouragement to not participate. Because of the campaign, hospice and pain-management are well-known in Oregon, and will be used as an alternative in many more cases. Because of this campaign, physicians have been called to be more responsive to the real needs of the terminally ill."

Sequel

Within days after the confirmation of the vote, which, on its face, had legalized physician-assisted suicide, a major happening occurred which apparently nullified the law. It came from a federal bureau in Washington. There is a non-political, medical branch of the government called the Drug Enforcement Administration (DEA). This is the branch that issues narcotic licenses to physicians. Each practicing physician must apply and receive an annual authorization to write prescriptions for morphine or other controlled substances. If and when this privilege is deemed to be abused by the DEA, it can and does summarily revoke that physician's license. This also applies to pharmacists. Such a license revocation is not like a criminal proceeding that needs proof beyond reasonable doubt. It is an administrative action, and the "offending" physician or pharmacist is guilty until proven innocent.

It was under this authority that the DEA, shortly after the passage of the law, issued a clarifying directive clearly instructing physicians as follows. It stated that if a physician prescribed a lethal dose of medicine for the purpose of assisting a patient in dying, that physician's license would be automatically revoked. The prescription, as required by Oregon law, would have to state in writing the reason for this lethal medication. A pharmacist receiving the prescription then not only could in conscience refuse to give out this medicine, but, the DEA announced, would have his or her license revoked if the pharmacist did give out that medication. This was done under the authority of a federal statute entitled The Controlled Substance Act. This in effect completely nullified the Oregon law.

The U.S. Congress, House and Senate, had earlier passed a law forbidding the use of any federal funds, through any program, to be used in aiding or abetting physician-assisted suicide. This had passed by an almost unanimous vote in both Houses. At the time of this writing, we are aware of moves being made in the U.S. Congress to back up the DEA regulation with a federal statute.

Conclusion

At first consideration, it would seem that the Oregon law, as passed, might be a landmark happening pointing toward future legalization of euthanasia elsewhere. The sobering fact was that this law was definitively passed after the Australian Parliament reversed the pro-euthanasia law passed by its Northern Territory; after the U.S. Supreme Court decision, detailed in Chapter X, and everything that was learned through this experience; and in the face of the progressive weakening of restraints on direct euthanasia in the Netherlands. All this would seem to point to this being a seminal happening.

Upon critical examination, however, it probably rather falls into the situation of being a unique happening. Many of the dynamics that led to this vote will not be repeated in other states or nations. What we must do is study this situation, but in the unique context in which it occurred.

Far more important to this ongoing saga of the "culture of death" will be continuing study of the ongoing deterioration in the Netherlands, of the remarkable total reversal by the select committee of the British House of Lords, of the reversal of the Northern Territory law in Australia, and of the overwhelming and brilliant arguments put forth before the U.S. Supreme Court.

Rather than leading the way to a cosmic change, the Oregon experience may someday be looked upon as a tragic happening, yes, but not a significant turning point in history. If this opinion is viewed as a bit of editorial wishful thinking by your authors, let it be so. But history will continue to unfold, and none of us can foresee exactly what the future holds.

CHAPTER XI

THE ANSWER
– COMPASSIONATE CARE –

Our concern here is not with the sudden death, the accident, the stroke, the heart attack. Rather, it is with those who die more slowly. The thrust of our discussion has been that suicide is not the answer. What, then, are answers?

First, one must realistically admit that dying, with some exceptions, is difficult. It is not usually pretty. It can be unpleasant, nothing to enjoy, and often times burdensome. But every person must someday tread that path into the Great Beyond. That person may someday be your parents, your spouse, your children or grandchildren, your dear friends, your loved ones, and, of course, one day yourself. Our task, if possible, is to make this passage as comfortable as it can be made, as meaningful, as fulfilling and peaceful as it can be made. Our task also is to leave those persons around the dying one with good memories, loving memories, and a sense of peace and acceptance.

Easy to do? Not really. But it can be done, and it behooves each of us to try. Most are familiar with the stages that a person goes through after they are confronted with that edict that the end of their worldly existence is coming. Hopefully, there are supportive persons around - ideally spouse, children, family - but otherwise friends and, at the very least, professionals in a hospice or equivalent setting. They must give support to this person, as he or she slowly deals with and accepts the reality of what is to come.

Fear, depression, anger, despair, loneliness are all part of this. Certainly physical symptoms and pain will aggravate it, and we have discussed this in depth earlier. The medical team must see to the fact that the patient remains reasonably comfortable physically. But that may well be the easy part. The difficult, but potentially most fulfilling part, then, lies ahead. Hopefully, with support and help from others, the dying person can get past her anger and come to the point of accepting that she will die, come to the point of losing her fear of the loss of personal control of her existence. The macho man and the independent woman must accept the fact that they are becoming dependent on others, something that often is an entirely new experience as, for many, they've never allowed themselves to be dependent in the past.

With this, then, often comes a feeling of uselessness – a knowledge that they will become "a burden" to others and a pervasive, continuing fear of this slowly developing, slowly changing, slowly progressing different existence.

What, then, lies ahead? A clamming up, a shutting out of the world? Despair? Hopefully not, for there is so much to do before each one of us dies. None of us has led a perfect life. Through our lifetime we have made mistakes, and we have done many things that we have regretted. Ofttimes, these actions have been directed at or were directly related to those closest to us – a spouse, a parent, a child, a sibling, a close friend or someone who once was close. In each of our lives we have left behind people who have been hurt, as we too have been – misunderstandings, resentments, buried anger.

But we have also, during our lifetime, often in so many ways taken for granted those who cared for us, who have helped us, who have done us so many favors, who have worked with us, who have loved us. To these, how often have we said, "Thank you"?

And then, of course, there are the very practical arrangements. How does one arrange for the disposition of his or her earthly goods? This certainly includes finances, but it also includes so much more – those pieces of china that her daughter so loves, Dad's old cane, the piano, pieces of her jewelry (valuable or not), other family or professional mementos. What of all of these? She won't be needing them anymore. Now is a time to perhaps share them with her loved ones.

Without question, for many or most, there is a need for spiritual reconciliation, pondering, praying, and an attempt to make things right with the Lord.

Many people will say they hope that, when they go, they go quickly. But many of us, experienced in terminal care, would not share that. Rather, we see value to that time at the end. There is a five-point commentary for those familiar with hospice care. These are a marvelous way of stating what one's end can be like. Hospice calls them "the five things of relationship completion". They are "I forgive you – forgive me – thank you – I love you – goodbye."

Hospice care, or its equivalent, properly accomplished, lovingly and professionally done, is without question modern society's answer to euthanasia. Hospice is usually a building, an institution, but its services are not confined to four walls. More patient hospice care occurs at home, on visits to nursing homes and in other settings than actually occurs within the walls of a hospice. It is a wonderful place to go to die. An acute hospital is too often a lousy place to die. An acute hospital is too often noisy, the lights never go out, the patient next to you keeps you awake, you're constantly being bothered to have your temperature taken, your blood pressure checked or meals to eat. There are problems with visiting hours, and the list goes on.

A hospice is an approximation of the ideal situation of dying at home. In a hospice, there are no heroic efforts to prolong a life. When life naturally ebbs and slips away, that is accepted, not fought against. In a hospice, there is an expertise available for pain control. That, above all, is taken care of.

In a hospice, visiting hours are whenever your loved ones want to come. They can stay as long as they like. Visitors can and should participate in the care of the patient – feeding, bathing, oiling, rubbing, singing, talking, praying, listening. This is a place where grandchildren can come and even bring their pets. This is a place where clergy are not merely squeezed into a busy schedule, not merely tolerated, but accepted as an integral part of the team. This is a place from which the patient can leave to go home, if his or her condition improves for a time. This is a place where you look out the window at a sylvan setting and not at a powerhouse or parking lot.

Hospice provides a team approach. Doctors, professional nurses, yes, but social workers, clergy, physiotherapists and, above all, the gift of time. Does that busy, efficient professional nurse in the hospital have time to sit down and just talk, or, more importantly, to just listen to the patient? Rarely. But in a hospice, that is her job. As it turns out, a particular patient has an estranged brother in a distant city but no nearby family to make that contact. In a hospital, very likely nothing is done. In a hospice, that *is* what they're all about. They will contact him and urge him to come to visit, to talk, to share before his sister dies.

In a hospice, all of the various workings out at the end of life that are described and touched upon in this chapter are most emphatically *the* business of the hospice. The emphasis upon living with dignity until death and the very special and compassionate way of truly caring for a patient in the most complete fashion physically, emotionally and spiritually – that *is* the business of hospice. If you have a hospice available to you, you are fortunate. If you do not, perhaps some of you might become involved in setting up a hospice in your community. If not, then perhaps each of you, when that opportunity is presented to you, may attempt to do your part in being a one-person hospice to your loved one who is dying

With knowledge of the above being hopefully available, let us then look further at how the time of dying can be a rich and fulfilling time.

Substantial personal growth can occur while approaching death and, literally yet, while dying. Dying, in that sense, can be a time of personal fulfillment to the patient but also to those around him.

This can be a time to complete such as the following:

• A son, long estranged from his father for perhaps, in his mind, justifiably good reasons. The father is near death. That son can come back and, forgetting who was guilty of what, can tell his father that he loves him and ask for his father's forgiveness insofar as he himself was in the wrong. A father's response in such an instance is usually one of embracing him whom he sees as a prodigal son. Such an exchange of love, very likely with tears, can release both from the emotional bondage of long-harbored anger and resentment, but also can alleviate personal guilt.

• A grandfather can gather grandchildren about him and recall for them tales of his earlier life, of his own boyhood and growing up, of how he met their grandmother, their courtship and marriage, their bearing and rearing of the parents of these children. Stories such as these, often heard for the first time by these little ones, will not be forgotten. They offer a bridge to the past, a tie in blood between generations, a pride of "ownership" in having had this grandpa. This also serves as a positive and loving example to these children's parents, and to the children themselves, of the inter-generational role that grandparents can and should play, and that hopefully each of them will play someday.

• A divorced wife, long estranged from her husband, carrying with her, as does he, a wall of bitterness from that painful separation experience. Deep inside both of them, completely unspoken and fully repressed (most of the time), there usually yet remains some feelings of regret, of perhaps not having put forth the full effort each could have to preserve that union, of perhaps even being somewhat ashamed of oneself for having done or said some of the things that led up to that break. All of these can add up, deep inside of each, to unresolved emotional feelings. If she can come to this dying man, embrace him, tell him how she remembers their initial love and that some of that still remains in her heart, tell him she's sorry for whatever hurts she has caused him and ask him to forgive her. Almost certainly the wall between them will dissolve. He will accept, forgive and respond to her in kind. Now all of the facade, the built-up incrustations of time, the pride, the self-justifications fade away. In such a tender moment, the result can often be that he can die in peace, that she knows it, and that she herself can go back to her own life with a lighter heart, a cleaner conscience, a burden lifted from her soul, and a peace of soul.

• This can be a time of clearing one's spiritual conscience of guilt and sin, to share time with a priest who can offer forgiveness in the Sacrament of Confession, to share time with a minister or with a rabbi to discuss and relieve one's soul and to be reassured of God's forgiveness of past sins. To share such a time with a trusted friend. This is a time to open a locked conscience and get such previous violations of God's rules (as he or she sees them) cleared from one's conscience.

• An example seen in recent years might be that of a son who had left his family to lead the life of a homosexual, to acquire AIDS and to come home to die. Hopefully, he will be received by his family with forgiveness, with love and with care. If his conscience and value system so leads him, this could be an opportunity to ask for understanding – yes, and for forgiveness – from those whom he had left. Again a possibility, then, of bringing, both to him and his family, a degree of reconciliation, of sharing of love and of peace of soul.

• For any and all such reunions it can be a time for a one-on-one – talking, listening, explaining, understanding and sharing. It can be a time of frank exchange of feelings, of why and how this happened, and then of a mutual understanding that none of this really matters anymore. It's a time of following up those five acts of the Hospice Code which can be repeated in varying degrees with each of those loved ones with whom such a meeting occurs.

Memories are powerful things. They follow us our entire life. We have our share of bitter ones, of angry ones, of just plain bad memories. It is not good to bury those bad memories. It is much better for them to surface in an atmosphere where love can be exchanged and mutual forgiveness is relatively easy to extend. When we strip away all of the encumbrances of modern life – of money, of prestige, of power, of pride – the important things that remain at the very end are our relationship to people, primarily to our own flesh and blood, to those we have loved, those who are closest to us. It is so much better to bury good memories than bad ones.

Conclusion

Your author and many others who have cared for dying persons hope that each of you, when confronted with a person who is dying, will try to make those last weeks and days a time to remember, a time of fulfillment, a time to consider once again those five last acts:

I forgive you . . . Forgive me . . . Thank you . . . I love you . . . Goodbye

BIBLIOGRAPHY

Dying Well – The Prospect for Growth at the End of Life, by Ira Byock, M.D., President of American Academy of Hospice & Palliative Medicine – ISBN 1-57322-051-5 – 1997 – Hardbound – US $24.95 – Heart-touching cases of compassionate care

When Death Is Sought – Assisted Suicide & Euthanasia in the Medical Context, by the New York State Task Force on Life & the Law – ISBN 1-881268-01-2 – 1994 – Available from New York State Task Force on Life & the Law, 5 Penn Plaza, New York, NY 10001-1803 – A comprehensive official examination

Issues in Law & Medicine, Verbatum, The Glucksberg & Quill Amicus Curiae Briefs, Condensation by Richard Coleson, JD, Vol. 13, No. 1 – Summer 1997 – National Legal Center for the Medically Dependent & Disabled, P.O. Box 1586, Terre Haute, IN 47808-1586 – Almost indispensable, unless you want to read all 51 briefs.

A Grave Danger – Physician-Assisted Suicide – Reprint of Duquesne Law Review, Vol. 38, 1. – 1996 – Pittsburgh Leadership Foundation Press, 100 Ross Street, Pittsburgh, PA 15219 – Excellent analyses leading up to U.S. Supreme Court decision

The Threat of Euthanasia, Proceedings, First International Conference on Life-Threatening Euthanasia in Holland and Abroad – 1996 – ISBN 90-71732-05-3 – Available from Schreeuw om Leven, Hilversum, Ruitersweg 35-37, 1211 KT Hilversum, The Netherlands. – Also – Second International Conference, ISBN 90-71732-05-3, Hilversum, June 16-19, 1996

Seduced By Death – Doctors, Patients & the Dutch Cure,
Herbert Hendin, M.D., Executive Director of American Suicide
Foundation, ISBN 0-393-04003-8, W. W. Norton & Company –
1996 – Hardbound – $27.50 US
– Details the Dutch experience

Death As A Salesman – What's Wrong With Assisted Suicide, Brian
Johnston, ISBN 0-9641125-0-7 – New Regency Publishing – 1994,
Paper – $10.95 US
– Extensive detail about J. Kevorkian and victims

R. Marker, *Deadly Compassion*, ISBN 0-688-12221-3,
W. Morrow & Co., 1993. Details on Hemlock Society, Derek Humphrey
and death of Ann Humphrey

J. E. Tada, *When Is It Right To Die?*, Zondervan, 1992,
ISBN 0-310-58570-0, by a Christian who is disabled

FOOTNOTES

CHAPTER II FOOTNOTES

[1] See James Rachels, *The End of Life* 77 (1986) (acknowledging that euthanasia is less about autonomy than about societal recognition that certain human beings lack sufficient human attributes to possess lives); Peter Singer, *Bioethics and Academic Freedom*, Bioethics (1990); John Harris, *Euthanasia and the Value of Life*, Euthanasia Examined: Ethical, Clinical and Legal Perspectives 6 (J. Keown ed. 1995).

[2] Derr, *supra*, 8 Issues in Law & Med. at 488. See also Proctor, *Racial Hygiene, supra* at 282-83; Lifton, *The Nazi Doctors, supra* at 45-51; Burleigh, *Death and Deliverance, supra* at 11-20.

[3] Proctor, *Racial Hygiene, supra* at 178-79.

[4] Wetham, *The Geranium in the Window*, (1966), reprinted in Death, Dying & Euthanasia at 610-611 (D. Horan & D. Mall, eds. 1980); Lifton, *The Nazi Doctors, supra* at 45-58.

[5] 8 Issues in Law & Med. at 232.

[6] *Id.* at 247-49. As to this last group, Binding expressed doubt that "a standard procedure can be created for managing this group of killings. Cases will occur in which killing seems actually fully justified; but it can also happen that the agent, in the belief that he acted correctly, acted precipitously." *Id.* at 250.

[7] *Id.* at 258.

[8] In general, euthanasia as described by Binding and Hoche and their German predecessors had a societal and statist component that distinguished it from the American tradition of individual rights, to which the current euthanasia movement adheres. See Lifton,*The Nazi Doctors, supra* at 47. The distinction, however, may be more sharp in theory than in practice. Contemporary euthanasia proponents do not rely exclusively on the autonomy of those whose lives would be ended,

but on the notion that such persons have ceased to have a "life". See Rachels, Singer and Harris, *supra* note 4. In the Netherlands, moreover, most physician-assisted deaths occur without the explicit request of the patient. See Brief *Amicus Curiae* of the American Suicide Foundation in No. 96-110.'

[9] 8 Issues in Law & Med. at 262. As for the third category, Binding considered as proper candidates those who "would (had they not fallen into unconsciousness at the critical time or if they had been able to achieve awareness of the situation) have requested or consented." 8 Issues in Law & Med. at 250.'

[10] *Id.* (Emphasis in original.)

[11] *Id.* at 252.

[12] Burleigh, *Death and Deliverance, supra* at 24.

[13] *Id. supra* at 15.

[14] *Id.* at 21.

[15] Burleigh, *Death and Deliverance, supra* at 21-22 (citations omitted).

[16] Lifton, *The Nazi Doctors, supra* at 48.

[17] *Id.* at 22-44.

[18] See Burleigh, *Death and Deliverance, supra* at 183-219.

[19] *Id.* at 204 (quotation from film).

[20] *Id.'* at 201-05 (quotations from films).

[21] One of the persons involved in these physician-assisted death programs was Alfons Klein, supervisor at Hadamar sanitorium. His attorney described the course of events leading up to the whole slaughter: In a motion picture called, "I Accuse," the problem of euthanasia, that is, mercy killing, was expounded. This picture was simply a prelude for things to come, because shortly after the beginning of the war the government passed a law whereby people who were afflicted mentally should be put out of the way . . . from January 1941 to July 1945, more than 10,000 German mental patients were killed in Hadamar alone. (*The Hadamar Trial*, infra at 220-21). Counsel for Hadamar defendant Dr. Adolf Wahlamann further described what was to happen in the elite German Medical Community: The opinion was held in important circles that people of so low a physical or mental standard that their lives were not worth living, and for whom there was no hope of recovery or ability to work, should be removed after medical examination, especially when they themselves were a burden on their

relatives and on the general public . . . In Germany, this point of view was put before the public through the media of books and movies, and was gradually recognized by widening circles. (*The Hadamar Trial*, infra at 226.)

[22] *Brandt*, Nurem. Mil. Trib., infra at 877-80; Kamisar, *Non-Religious Views*, *supra* pra at 470; Gallagher, *By Trust Betrayed*, *supra* at 69 (Viktor Brack maintained that "the blessing of euthanasia should be granted only to [true] Germans"). '

[23] Derr, *supra*, 8 Issues in Law & Med. at 494.

[24] *Id.* at 488-89. "It would be a mistake to call it a Nazi program. It was not. The program was conceived by physicians and operated by them. They did the killing." Gallagher, *By Trust Betrayed*, *supra* at 5.

[25] Gallagher, *By Trust Betrayed*, *supra* at 60.

[26] Proctor, *Racial Hygiene*, *supra* at 193; see also Gallagher, *supra* at 5, 46.

[27] Proctor, *Racial Hygiene*, *supra* at 182.

[28] Proctor, *Racial Hygiene*, *supra* at 186; Burleigh, *Death and Deliverance*, *supra* at 93-96.

[29] Gallagher, *By Trust Betrayed*, *supra* at 47; Proctor, *Racial Hygiene*, *supra* at 186.

[30] Alexander Mitscherlich, *The Death Doctors* (1962) (James Cleugh, trans.) at 234.

[31] Burleigh, *Death and Deliverance*, *supra* at 98. Few parents, however, were as explicit as a woman who requested that the Ministry of Interior "have her two "idiot children' taken to the asylum at Schleswig in order to carry out euthanasia." *Id.* at 102.

[32] *Id.* at 111; Lifton, *The Nazi Doctors*, *supra* at 50, 56.

[33] Burleigh, *Death and Deliverance*, *supra* at 93.

[34] Henry Friedlander, *The Origins of Nazi Genocide: From Euthanasia to the Final Solution* 171-72 (1995).

[35] Proctor, *Racial Hygiene*, *supra* at 186.

[36] *Id.* at 194.

[37] Friedlander, *The Origins of Nazi Genocide*, *supra* at 300.

[38] *United States v. Brandt et al., Trials of War Criminals Before the Nuremberg Military Tribunals Under Control Council Law No. 10*, Nuremberg, October 1946-April 1947, Vol. II:196.

[39] Proctor, *Racial Hygiene*, *supra* at 193; Burleigh, *Death and*

Deliverance, *supra* at 98-99.

[40] Proctor, *Racial Hygiene, supra* at 193.

[41] Proctor, *Racial Hygiene, supra* at 190.

[42] Lifton, *The Nazi Doctors, supra* at 138-39.

[43] Lifton, *The Nazi Doctors, supra at 54; Burleigh, Death and Deliverance, supra* at 101. These hospitals and health care facilities included Wurtemberg, Brandenburg, Hartheim, Sonnenstein, Hadamar, Leipzig-Dosen, Eglfing-Haar, Meseritz-Obrawalde, Tiegenhof, Langenhorn, Bernburg, Eichberg, Kalmenhof, Uchtspringe, Konigslutter, Scheunern, Mainkofen, Am Steinhof, and Kaufbeuren. Friedlander, *The Origins of Nazi Genocide, supra* at 87-89, 95, 152-53, and 162. In fact, the killing secretly continued at Kaufbeuren, Eglfing-Haar, and a few other hospitals for months after the war ended and Allied forces assumed control. Gallagher, *By Trust Betrayed, supra* at 249-50.

[44] Lifton, *The Nazi Doctors, supra* at 72.

[45] Proctor, *Racial Hygiene, supra* at 189-90.

[46] Lifton, *The Nazi Doctors, supra* at 71.

[47] *The Hadamar Trial: Proceedings of a Military Commission for the Trial for War Criminals*, Introduction at xxiv (E. Kintner ed. 1948). Counsel for Hadamar physician Adolf Wahlmann insisted at his war crimes trial, "In general, the people killed were those faced with a permanent illness, for whom a completely painless death was a relief," *The Hadamar Trial, supra* at 228. "Insane people are useless to society and as a rule do not endure pain. . . . Incurable tubercular patients, on the other hand, have to suffer terrific pain," added counsel for Heinrich Ruoff. *Id.* at 233.

[48] *Id.* at 69-70.

[49] Lifton, *The Nazi Doctors, supra at 192; Burleigh, Death and Deliverance, supra* at 160.

[50] The Hadamar Trial, supra at Introduction xxiv.

[51] Lifton, *The Nazi Doctors, supra* at 255.

[52] Lifton, *The Nazi Doctors, supra* at 134-44; Burleigh, *Death and Deliverance, supra* at 132-33.

[53] Friedlander, *The Origins of Nazi Genocide, supra* at 150; Lifton, *The Nazi Doctors, supra* at 142.

[54] Alexander, *Medical Science Under Dictatorship, supra* 241 New Eng.

J. Med. at 45-46.

[55] Lifton, *The Nazi Doctors, supra* at 142.

[56] On Jan. 20, 1942, nearly four years after the euthanasia program for Germans began with the *gnadentod* of the Knauer child, the plans for the Final Solution of the "Jewish Problem" were completed at the Wannsee Conference, a meeting of 13 high-ranking government officials. Proctor, *Racial Hygiene, supra* at 210; Lifton, *The Nazi Doctors, supra* at 158. Even then, "during early 1942, the details of the killing procedure were not yet clear, and were not solved until spring with the establishment of gas chamber camps in Poland." Lifton, *The Nazi Doctors, supra* at 158.

[57] Burleigh, *Death and Deliverance, supra* at 277.

[58] *Id.* at 100.

[59] Burleigh, *Death and Deliverance, supra* at 273.

[60] Nurem. Mil. Trib. II:139.

[61] *The Hadamar Trial, supra* at 88.

[62] Burleigh, *Death and Deliverance, supra* at 152, 160.

[63] *Id.* at 289.

[64] Nurem. Mil. Trib. I:66-71.

[65] Alexander, *supra*, 241 New Eng. J. Med. at 44. In the last year of his life, Dr. Alexander drew explicit links between the German experience he had studied so extensively and the advocacy for legalized euthanasia in the United States: "It is much like Germany in the 20's and 30's. The barriers against killing are coming down." Patrick G. Derr, "The Real Brophy Issue," *The Boston Globe* 15 (Nov. 18, 1985).

[66] *Id.*

[67] 8 Issues in Law & Med. at 265.

[68] *Id.* at 254.

CHAPTER VI FOOTNOTES

[1]   Personal communication to author

[2]   K. Gunning, President of World Federation of Doctors Who Respect Life, Rotterdam, 16 Sept. 1997

[3]   K. Haasnoot, Euth. Developments in the Netherlands, 2nd International Conference on Euthanasia, Hilversum, Holland, June 16-19, 1996, Pg. 21

[4]   J. Keown, *Some Reflections on Euthanasia in the Netherlands*; in Euthanasia, Clinical Practice & the Law, 1994, 198-201

[5]   "Remmelink" Report by Dutch Government Committee, Sept. 10, 1991. R. Fenigsen, *Issues of Law & Medicine*, Vol. 7, No. 3, Winter 1991, Pg. 339

[6a] Euthanasia . . . Netherlands 1990-95, P. Van der Maas et al, *New England Journal of Medicine*, Vol. 335, No. 22, Nov. 28, 1996, Pg. 1699-1705

[6b] *Evaluation of Notification Procedure*, Netherlands, G. Van der Wal et al, *New England Journal of Medicine*, Vol. 335, No. 22, Nov. 28, '96, Pg. 1706-1711

[7]   *Physician Assisted Suicide & Euthanasia in the Netherlands, Lessons from the Dutch*, H. Hendin et al, JAMA, June 4, 1997, Vol. 277, No. 21, Pgs. 1720-22

[8]   See Keown above

[9]   Personal communication to author

[10] Assen Case, Dutch Supreme Court, June 1994, re Dr. Chabot

[11] *C. Gomez, Regulating Death: Euthanasia and the Ease of the Netherlands*, 1991, Pg. 110

[12] Personal communication to author

[13] Personal communication to author

CHAPTER VII FOOTNOTES

[1] *Does It Make Clinical Sense To Equate Terminally Ill Patients Who Require Life-sustaining Interventions With Those Who Do Not? –* L.A. Alpers & B. Lo, *JAMA*, June 4, 1997, Vol. 277, No. 21, Pg. 1705-08

[2] *Pain Management, Challenging the Myths*, J. Anderson, *Med. World News*, April 1992, Pg. 20

[3] E. Robbins, *The Final Months*, 12 (1991)

[4] *A Hundred Cases of Suicide*, Barraclough et al, 125 *British Journal of Psychiatry*, 1976, Pg. 355-56

[5] *Assisted Suicide in Medical Ethics: In the Patient's Best Interests? –* E. Pellegrino, Mar. 7, 1997, Columbus School of Law, Washington D.C.

CHAPTER VIII FOOTNOTES

[1] Select Committee on Medical Ethics of the British House of Lords

[2] Report of the Select Committee on medical ethics of the House of Lords, Vol. I, London, 31 Jan. 1994. Excerpts –

VOLUNTARY EUTHANASIA

236. The right to refuse medical treatment is far removed from the right to request assistance in dying. We spent a long time considering the very strongly held and sincerely expressed views of those witnesses who advocated voluntary euthanasia. Many of us have had experience of relatives or friends whose dying days or weeks were less than peaceful or uplifting, or whose final stages of life were so disfigured that the loved one seemed already lost to us, or who were simply weary of life. Our thinking must inevitably be coloured by such experience. The accounts we received from individual members of the public about such experiences were particularly moving, as were the letters from those who themselves longed for the release of an early death. Our thinking must also be coloured by the wish of every individual for a peaceful and easy death, without prolonged suffering, and by a reluctance to contemplate the possibility of severe dementia or dependence. We gave much thought too to Professor Dworkin's opinion that, for those without religious belief, the individual is best able to decide what manner of death is fitting to the life which has been lived.

237. Ultimately, however, we do not believe that these arguments are sufficient reason to weaken society's prohibition of intentional killing. That prohibition is the cornerstone of law and of social relationships. It protects each one of us impartially, embodying the belief that all are equal. We do not wish that protection to be diminished and we therefore recommend that there should be no change in the law to permit euthanasia. We acknowledge that there are individual cases in which euthanasia may be seen by some to be appropriate. But individual cases cannot reasonably establish the foundation of a policy which would have such serious and widespread repercussions. Moreover dying is not only a personal or individual affair. The death of a person affects the lives of others, often in ways and to an extent which cannot be foreseen. We believe that the issue of euthanasia is one in which the interest of the individual cannot be separated from the interest of society as a whole.

238. One reason for this conclusion is that we do not think it possible to set secure limits on voluntary euthanasia. Some witnesses told us that to legalise voluntary euthanasia was a discrete step which need

have no other consequences. But as we said in our introduction, issues of life and death do not lend themselves to clear definition, and without that it would not be possible to frame adequate safeguards against non-voluntary euthanasia if voluntary euthanasia were to be legalised. It would be next to impossible to ensure that all acts of euthanasia were truly voluntary, and that any liberalisation of the law was not abused. Moreover to create an exception to the general prohibition of intentional killing would inevitably open the way to its further erosion whether by design, by inadvertence, or by the human tendency to test the limits of any regulation. These dangers are such that we believe that any decriminalisation of voluntary euthanasia would give rise to more and more grave problems than those it sought to address. Fear of what some witnesses referred to as a "slippery slope" could in itself be damaging.

239. We are also concerned that vulnerable people – the elderly, lonely, sick or distressed – would feel pressure, whether real or imagined, to request early death. We accept that, for the most part, requests resulting from such pressure or from remediable depressive illness would be identified as such by doctors and managed appropriately. Nevertheless we believe that the message which society sends to vulnerable and disadvantaged people should not, however obliquely, encourage them to seek death, but should assure them of our care and support in life.

240. Some of those who advocated voluntary euthanasia did so because they feared that lives were being prolonged by aggressive medical treatment beyond the point at which the individual felt that continued life was no longer a benefit but a burden. But, in the light of the consensus which is steadily emerging over the circumstances in which life-prolonging treatment may be withdrawn or not initiated, we consider that such fears may increasingly be allayed. We welcome moves by the medical professional bodies to ensure more senior oversight of practice in casualty departments, as a step towards discouraging inappropriately aggressive treatment by less experienced practitioners.

241. Furthermore, there is good evidence that, through the outstanding achievements of those who work in the field of palliative care, the pain and distress of terminal illness can be adequately relieved in the vast majority of cases. Such care is available not only within hospices, thanks to the increasing dissemination of best practice by means of home-care teams and training for general practitioners, palliative care is becoming more widely available in the health service,

147

in hospitals and in the community, although much remains to be done. With the necessary political will such care could be made available to all who could benefit from it. We strongly commend the development and growth of palliative care services.'

[3] Brief of Am. Med. Assn., Am. Nurses Assn., Am. Psychiatric Assn. et al in *State of Washington v. Glucksberg*, Nov. 12, 1996, #96-110, from AMA, 515 N. State St., Chicago, IL 60610

[4] Brief by the above in *Vacco v. Quill*, Nov. 12, 1996, #95-1858

[5] In addition to the AMA, the following 51 organizations signed on to the friend-of-the-court brief to the U.S. Supreme Court in opposition to physician-assisted suicide: American Nurses Assn., American Assn. of Critical-Care Nurses, Hospice Nurses Assn., Oncology Nurses Society, American Osteopathic Assn., American Psychiatric Assn., American Academy of Hospice & Palliative Medicine, American Academy of Pain Management, American Academy of Pain Medicine, American Academy of Orthopaedic Surgeons, American Academy of Physical Medicine & Rehabilitation, Society of Critical Care Medicine, American Academy of Neurology, American Neurological Assn., American Society of Anesthesiologists, American Society of Clinical Pathologists, College of American Pathologists, American Society of Abdominal Surgeons, American Assn. of Clinical Endocrinologists, California Medical Assn., Medical Society of the State of New York, Medical Assns. of the State of Alabama, Arkansas Medical Society, Medical Assn. of Georgia, Illinois State Medical Society, Indiana State Medical Assn., Iowa Medical Society, Louisiana State Medical Society, Massachusetts Medical Society, Mississippi State Medical Assn., Missouri State Medical Assn., Montana Medical Assn., Nebraska Medical Assn., Medical Society of New Jersey, New Mexico Medical Society, North Carolina Medical Society, Ohio State Medical Assn., Tennessee Medical Assn., Texas Medical Assn., Vermont Medical Society, Medical Society of the State of Virginia, West Virginia Medical Assn., Society of Medical Consultants to the Armed Forces, American Institute of Life-Threatening Illness & Loss, National Hispanic Council on Aging.

[6a] *Assisted Suicide's Fate*, Am. Med. News, July 21, 1997, Pg. 33

[6b] *When Death Is Sought, NY State Task Force on Life & the Law*, May 1994, ISBN 1-881268-01-2

[7] This and subsequent briefs summarized in *Issues in Law & Medicine*, Vol. 13, No. 1, Summer 1997, Pub. Office, P.O. Box 1586, Terre Haute, IN 47808

CHAPTER IX FOOTNOTES

[1]   *Quill v. Vacco*, 80 F. 3d 716, 2nd Cir. 1996

[2]   *Washington v. Glucksberg*, 117 S. Ct. 37, 9th Cir. 1996